New Radical Enlightenment

New Radical Enlightenment

Philosophy for a Common World

Marina Garcés

Translated from Catalan
and Spanish by Julie Wark

VERSO

London • New York

This book was translated with the help of a
grant from the Institut Ramon Llull

LLLL institut
ramon llull

This English-language edition first published by Verso 2024
Translation © Julie Wark 2024
First published as *Nova il·lustració radical* and *Filosofía inacabada*
© Anagrama 2017 and Galaxia Gutenberg 2015

1 3 5 7 9 10 8 6 4 2

Verso
UK: 6 Meard Street, London W1F 0EG
US: 388 Atlantic Avenue, Brooklyn, NY 11217
versobooks.com

Verso is the imprint of New Left Books

ISBN-13: 978-1-83976-298-7
ISBN-13: 978-1-83976-299-4 (UK EBK)
ISBN-13: 978-1-83976-300-7 (US EBK)

British Library Cataloguing in Publication Data
A catalogue record for this book is available from the British Library

Library of Congress Cataloging-in-Publication Data
A catalog record for this book is available from the Library of Congress

Typeset in Sabon by MJ & N Gavan, Truro, Cornwall
Printed and bound by CPI Group (UK) Ltd, Croydon CR0 4YY

Contents

Preface

Today's world is radically anti-enlightenment. If Kant declared in 1784 that European societies were then in a time of Enlightenment, we could say that now, throughout the planet, we are in a time of anti-enlightenment. Kant used the term in a dynamic sense. The Enlightenment was not a state but a task. The same goes for our time. The anti-enlightenment is not a state but a war.

The faces of this anti-enlightenment war are many and multiplying by the day. In the political domain, a growing authoritarian impulse has turned despotism and violence into a new mobilising force. It is often called populism, but this is a confusing term. What we have is a new authoritarianism permeating society as a whole. In the cultural realm, defensive and offensive identities are triumphing. White Western Christianity is doubling down on its values while also unleashing anti-Western rage in many parts of the world, and even in Western critical thought, which rejects its own genealogy. In all quarters, fascination with the premodern is triumphing: everything that existed 'before' was better. As Zygmunt Bauman explains in his posthumous book *Retrotopia*, this is a search for refuge in utopias projected onto an idealised past, from tribal life to eulogising any form of precolonial life, for the mere fact of being so. Today, education, knowledge, and science are also falling into disrepute, from which they can escape only if they show that they are able to offer specific solutions to society: employment solutions, technical solutions, economic solutions.

Solutionism is the cover for knowledge that has lost the power to make us better, both as individuals and as a society. We no longer believe in knowledge, which is why we ask for solutions and nothing but solutions. We do not think about bettering ourselves but only about obtaining more and more privileges in a time that is going nowhere because it has given up aiming at a better future.

The anti-enlightenment war legitimises a social, cultural, and political regime that is based on voluntary credulousness. In his famous essay *What Is Enlightenment?*, Kant speaks of man's 'self-incurred immaturity'. Today, instead of this 'minority of age' (*Minderjährigheit*), what we have is an adult – or, rather, senile – society that is cynically willing to believe or pretend to believe whatever is in its best interest at any given time. The media call this post-truth, but this is also a 'retrotopian' term because it suggests that truth is what we have left behind, in some better past. There was not more truth or less truth in the past. Rather, there are different ways of combatting the credulity that oppresses people in different epochs. We need to find our own particular way of combatting the system of credulousness in our own time. Our present impotence has a name: enlightened illiteracy. We know everything but can do nothing. With all of humanity's knowledge at our beck and call, we can only slow down or speed up our fall into the abyss.

The radical Enlightenment was a battle against credulousness, trusting that human nature could become emancipated and improve itself. Its weapon: criticism. We must not confuse this radically critical option with the project of modernisation which, with the expansion of capitalism and by means of colonialism, has dominated the world for the last three centuries. There is a gap between the 'civilising' project of domination and the critical option of emancipation, which needs to be explored anew. After the Second World War, Adorno and Horkheimer wrote their famous epitaph on the present in *Dialectic of Enlightenment*: 'Enlightenment, understood in the widest sense as the advance of thought, has always aimed at liberating human beings from fear and installing them as masters. Yet the wholly enlightened earth is radiant with triumphant calamity."*

Ever since then, Enlightenment and calamity have been understood as almost synonymous terms. But this identification contains another one: 'liberating human beings from fear and installing them as masters' is asserted to be the same thing. But is that really the case? Given the present magnitude of the calamity, which has brought the human species itself to the limits of sustainability, perhaps the time has come to unravel the implications of this statement and this twofold identification. That all liberation leads to even more terrible forms of domination, and that every form of knowledge mobilises new power relations are truisms but so, too, is the reactionary argument used to condemn any radical project to transform the world and to encourage the personal and collective desire for emancipation. We have therefore come to accept as dogma the irreversibility of catastrophe. And this is why, beyond modernity – which designed a future for everyone – and post-modernity – which celebrated an inexhaustible present for each person – our epoch is that of the posthumous condition. We survive, pitted against each other, in a time that only subtracts.

What if we dared to think, once again, about the relationship between knowledge and emancipation? They seem to be hackneyed, naïve words, but this is precisely the demobilising effect that the powers-that-be are pursuing today as they ridicule our capacity for educating ourselves so we can construct, together, a more habitable and just world. We are offered all kinds of salvation gadgets, in the form of technology and discourse on demand. Leaders and flags. Acronyms. Bombs. This sets us off on projects of delegated intelligence, in which we can finally

* Max Horkheimer and Theodor W. Adorno, *Dialectic of Enlightenment: Philosophical Fragments*, trans. Edmund Jeffcott, Stanford, CA: Stanford University Press, 2002, p. 1.

be as stupid as we humans have shown we are because the world and its leaders will be intelligent for us. A smart world for irremediably idiotic inhabitants.

We are no longer bogged down in the dialectics of enchantment and disenchantment which stained with shadows the culture of the nineteenth and twentieth centuries. We are on the verge of surrender: surrender of the human race in the face of the task of learning and educating ourselves in order to live with greater dignity. Faced with this surrender, I propose that we should think about a new radical enlightenment, resume the battle against credulousness, and affirm the freedom and dignity of the human experience in its capacity to learn from itself. In its day, this struggle was revolutionary. Now it is necessary. Then, its light shone as an expansive and promising, invasive, and dominating universal. Now, in the planetary era, we can learn to conjugate a reciprocal and welcoming universal.

An essay is writing in progress. Some threads in this essay have been developed in recent lectures like 'Unfinishing the World' (CCCB, Barcelona), 'Humanities in Transition' (Institute of Humanities, Barcelona), 'Really Useful Knowledge' (Museo Reina Sofía, Madrid), 'The Strength of Hunger' (MACBA, Barcelona), and 'The Posthumous Condition' (Mextrópoli, Mexico). They have also been shared and discussed with participants, whose involvement I am grateful for, in the Aula Oberta (Open Classroom) of the Humanities Institute of Barcelona, and in the Philosophy Seminar of the Juan March Foundation in Madrid. The resulting set of ideas is an advance on work to come.

Part I

New Radical Enlightenment

1

Our Posthumous Condition

Our time is the time of everything coming to an end. We are seeing the end of modernity, history, ideologies, and revolutions. We have been watching the end of progress: the future as a time of promise, development, and growth. Now we are seeing how basic resources like water, oil, and clean air are running out, and witnessing the demise of ecosystems and their biodiversity. In brief, our time is one when everything is ending, including time itself. This is not regression. Some say we are in a process of depletion or extinction. Maybe it will not come to that for us as a species, but it will for a civilisation based on development, progress, and expansion.

Routine press releases, academic debates, and the culture industry confront us with the need to think about ourselves from the standpoint that time is running out, and from the end of time. We are looking for exoplanets. The names of their discoverers are the new Columbuses and Marco Polos of the twenty-first century. Heroes in films are no longer conquering the Wild West but planet Mars. Some gullible people have already bought a departure ticket. The escape routes are being mapped out and the rich of this finite world are already queueing up.

In fact, the death of the future and of the idea of progress was announced quite a while ago, back in the 1980s when the future turned into an idea of the past, the stuff of the early enlightened ones, visionaries, and nostalgic revolutionaries. Globalisation promised an eternal present, an arrival point that developing countries would eventually reach, and where all of us citizens of the world would progressively become connected. But in recent times the end of history has been changing course. What we have before us now is not an eternal present or a place of arrival, but a threat. It has been said and written that, with 9/11, reality and history were set in motion again. But, instead of wondering where to, the question we ask ourselves today is for how long.

How long will I have a job? How long will I live with my partner? How long will pensions last? How long will Europe be white, secular, and rich? How long will there be potable water? How long will we keep believing in democracy? ... From the most intimate to the most collective questions, from individual to planetary, everything is done and undone in the shadow of a 'how long?' Even if history has been set in motion, we still have no future. What has changed is the relationship with the present, which has gone from being what had to last forever to what cannot last any longer. To what is literally unsustainable. This is how we live, hurtling into the time of imminence, in which everything can change radically, or everything can end definitively. It is hard to tell whether this imminence contains a revelation or a catastrophe. Fascination with the apocalypse dominates the political, aesthetic, and scientific scenes. It is a new, dominant ideology that must be isolated and analysed before, like a virus, it takes over the innermost recesses of our minds.

The impulse of 'now or never', or of 'if not now, when?' is stirring together with the question of 'how long?' From this impulse, current protest movements, self-organisation of life, intervention in wars, free culture, new feminisms ... are born. On both sides of the question, the same awareness is shared: this is not working or, in other words, it cannot keep going without collapsing. What is shared is the same experience of a limit. This is not any old limit but the limit of what is *liveable*. The threshold beyond which life might exist, but not for us, not human life. *Liveable* life: this is the big issue of our

4

time. Some think about it in mere terms of survival, even if it means scrambling out of this planet. Others among us go back to putting the old question on the table, or out in the streets: *liveable* life is one that is worth living. Its limits are those for which we can still struggle.

When people are now saying that time is running out and agree to keep heading for the irreversibility of our own death, what time and what death are being referred to? *Liveable* time, precisely. It is not abstract time, or empty time, but the time in which we can still intervene in our conditions of life. Faced with the expiry of *liveable* time and, ultimately, with anthropological breakdown, our time is no longer that of postmodernity but that of unsustainability. We are no longer in the postmodern condition that had blithely left the future behind, but in another experience of the end, the posthumous condition. Here, the *post-* does not signal what opens up after leaving behind the sweeping horizons and great references of modernity. Our *post-* is the one that comes *after* the after: a posthumous *post-*, extra time we give ourselves when we have envisioned and partly accepted the real possibility of our own end.

Unsustainability

The increasingly widespread awareness that 'this' (capitalism, economic growth, consumer society, productivism, or whatever you want to call it) is unsustainable radically questions the present state of affairs. That is why it is unmentionable. Or that is why its expression has been neutralised, for years now, with all sorts of terminological and ideological ruses. Since the 1970s, one of the main strategies for containing radical criticism of capitalism has been the concept of sustainability or, more specifically, sustainable development.

Sustainability appeared as a question or as a problem when the Club of Rome suggested, in its 1972 report *The Limits to Growth*, that, on a finite planet, unlimited growth is not possible. The question the report presented to the world also contained a 'how long?': how long could the planet as a whole – as a set of natural resources necessary for life – withstand, without collapse, the rate of exploitation and deterioration to which it was being submitted by the productive and vital activity of the human species?

The answer to this problem was sustainable development, pushed no longer as a contradiction to be resolved but as a solution to be put forward. As the 1987 *Brundtland Report* defined it, sustainable development was that which 'meets the needs of the present without compromising the ability of future generations to meet their own needs'. It is a concept that sparked a terminological dispute which was in fact a political conflict. As the economist José Manuel Naredo and others have explained, this clash led to intervention by none other than Henry Kissinger. The end result was an ideological armouring of any discussion about sustainability of the economic system itself. Neoliberalism was winning the battle of ideas and the imaginary which, to this very day, would dominate personal and collective desires across the planet. Including the environmental question by means of sustainability discourse neutralised any new challenges that might have arisen after the historic defeat of communism.

Since the crisis of 2008, what is seriously being called into question is precisely the sustainability of capitalism itself. The question that nourishes today's stories of apocalypse and the cancelling of the future points to the unlikely viability of an economic system based on growth and speculation. The question of 'how long?' does not only challenge the availability of natural resources and sources of energy. It goes further: how long will the capitalist system be able to keep going at this rate without the whole thing going pop? The question shifts from the planet and its limits to bubbles and their volatility. We are living on a finite planet that is on the verge of collapse, floating on bubbles (financial, real estate, and so on) that are about to burst.

Crisis is intrinsic to capitalism, as the classical economists, including Marx, pointed out. But what is now at stake is the very premise of growth as the condition for economic activity. The fact that in the eighteenth century growth was inseparable from political economy made some sense because that was what was being directly experienced: colonial expansion, exponential increases in wealth, technical leaps in industrialisation, population growth, and so on. However, now the perception is exactly the opposite. Why should we maintain a principle that contradicts our real experience of conditions of life today? This is the point at which a principle asserted by itself, against all evidence, becomes dogma. It is a dogma that, once again, hides behind the idea of sustainability. The sustainability that is now being preached is not only about natural resources but the economic system as such. The new slogan is 'Make the System Sustainable'. This has been the key argument of what are called austerity policies or, in other words, cuts in public spending and the privatisation of public services, especially in the south of Europe.

'Austerity' is one of the words presently being bandied around at the crossroads of the collective decisions of our time. Far from austerity as an ethical value, as an environmentally friendly anti-consumerist, pro-degrowth position, the austerity being evoked to ensure the sustainability of the system is, in fact, a machine that is used for cutting public spending and limiting expectations of a good life to the status of privilege. To put it more directly, this is a rearrangement of the parameters of a dignified life.

At this point, a new dimension of the question 'how long?' is opened up, now directly calling us into question, we human beings ourselves and our conditions of life. How long can we human beings withstand the conditions of life we have imposed on ourselves without falling apart (as individuals) or becoming extinct (as a species)? The question of sustainability which, in the 1970s, indicated the finiteness of the planet, now comes back to us like a boomerang, directly revealing our fragility and our own finiteness. We are then faced with a third experience of limits after that of the planet and that of the system, namely that of our own lives. This precariousness, which has become a recurring theme in philosophy, the arts, and the social and human sciences of our day, has many faces, and not all of them are easy bedfellows. They range from the psychological and physical malaise that plagues the wealthier societies through to the collapse of subsistence economies in the poorest ones. At both extremes, from soul to stomach, what is causing the suffering is a helplessness linked with the impossibility of dealing with and intervening in our own conditions of life. This is the end of *liveable* time, as I said at the start: a new feeling of despair.

It was announced as early as the 1950s by Günther Anders, for one, in his book of essays *The Obsolescence of Man*. What he suggested then was that humans had become small, but not small before the immensity of the world or under infinite skies, but small with regard to the consequences of their own actions. Anders was writing when technical rationality had produced and administered concentration camps and the atomic bomb. Yet he was not speaking only of this new capacity for programmed destruction but signalling an increasingly disturbing intuition that human action, both individual and collective, was not equal to the complexity it was generating and within which it would have to take place. The subject, as consciousness and will, has lost the ability to command action in the world and thus be the helmsperson of history. This intuition also presaged the defeat of the modern revolutionary cycle, with its drive to radically remake the world by means of political action. Since then, we have had a problem of scale that has placed us at the juncture of a painful contradiction: we are small and vulnerable, but we have inordinate power.

8

After Postmodernity

We have gone, then, from the postmodern condition to the posthumous condition. The meaning of an afterwards has changed: from the after-modernity to the after without an after. The civilisational consequences of this shift are being explored today, especially in literature, film and TV, and the arts. In its work on tracking future trends, fictional journalism, too, is devoting considerable attention to these changes. But how can we think about this? How can we think about it in such a way that understanding can take us beyond fear and resignation?

The postmodern condition was described by Jean-François Lyotard as disbelief in the great narratives and their effects on the sciences, language, and knowledge. In his account, what characterised postmodern forms of knowledge is the fact that history as a scenario of progress towards a more just society, and progress as a standpoint from which to assess scientific and cultural growth towards truth, were no longer frameworks for validating epistemological, cultural, and political activity. The postmodern afterwards, as Lyotard presents it in his *The Postmodern Condition: A Report on Knowledge*, is detached from the lineal sense of the historical metanarrative of progress and is opened up to multiple times, to heterochronies, to the value of interruption, to the event, and to discontinuities. As with punk, also yelling with life and rage in those years, the postmodern 'non-future' was experienced as liberation. In these circumstances, the posthumous condition looms over us with the imposition of a new single, lineal story: that of the irreversible destruction of our conditions of life. This inversion of the modern conception of history, characterised by the irreversibility of progress and revolution, now no longer holds in the future the fulfilment of history but its implosion. Historical linearity is back but it does not point to any light at the end of the tunnel but, rather, it blotches with shadows our showcases of unremitting artificial light.

9

This new narrative take on the sense of the future radically changes the experience of the present. In the 1980s and 1990s, economic globalisation invited humanity to celebrate an eternal present bloated with possibilities, simulacra, and promises to be fulfilled in the here and now. Postmodernity developed the meaning and tensions of this newfound temporality. Freed from the deadweight of the past and the alibi of the future, what globalisation held out was a never-ending present of hyper-consumption, of unlimited production, and of political unification of the world. It was a mercantile ecumenism that turned networks into a form of reconciliation and made of the terrestrial sphere the image of a saved community. In this present, a future was no longer needed because, somehow, it had been produced or was already in the pipeline.

What we are experiencing in the posthumous condition is not a return to the past or a major regression, as some present debates are suggesting we should think, but the breakdown of this eternal present, and the bringing about of a non-time. From a present of salvation to a present of condemnation. Our present is time running out. Every day is one day less. If the present of the postmodern condition was offered to us under the heading of forever-young earthly eternity, the present of the posthumous condition comes to us today under the heading of catastrophe on Earth and the sterility of life in common. Its time no longer calls for celebration but condemns us to vulnerability, depletion of natural resources, environmental destruction, and physical and spiritual malaise. From an endless party to time without a future.

The consequences of this shift go beyond analysis of temporality. They also have effects in how systems of power, identities, and even our sense of action are shaped. Postmodernity seemed to be the culmination of the biopolitical turn in modern politics. As Michel Foucault – followed by other authors from Giorgio Agamben to Antonio Negri – set out to analyse, after the eighteenth century the relationship between capitalism and the state gave rise to a biopolitical regime where management of individual and collective life was at the heart of legitimation of power and organisation of its practices of governability. It is not that there was no death decreed by the state's wartime or policing orders but, under the biopolitical regime, it was considered to be exceptional and a failing with regard to political normality. Nowadays, biopolitics is showing its necropolitical face. In management of life, the production of death is no longer seen as an exception or shortcoming but as normality. Terrorism, displaced populations, refugees, femicide, mass executions, suicides, famine from environmental causes … Non-natural death is not marginal or exceptional and neither does it disrupt the political order, but, rather, it has taken pride of place in democratic capitalist normality and its undeclared wars. Hobbes and the political order of modernity, where peace and war are the inside and outside of civilian life and state space, have been supplanted. So, too, has the Kantian vision of perpetual peace. In other words, the normative ideal of progress tending towards peace in the world has been erased from the map of our possibilities.

With these prospects, collective action (whether it is political, scientific, or technical) is no longer understood from the standpoint of experimentation but from that of emergency, as an operation of salvation, repair, or rescue. The most emblematic heroes of our time are the rescuers working the Mediterranean. Always willing to put their bodies on the line, to jump into the water to save a drifting life that has left behind a past and without any future, they represent the most radical action of our time. Saving a life, even if simply affirming that life, is its only horizon of meaning. Rescue as the only reward. Somehow, the 'new politics' that had emerged in Spain and that governed some towns, cities, and territories is presented as being in keeping with this logic. Rather than political transformation (which is to say, a future), its primary raison d'être is social emergency. Politics as an action of citizen rescue takes precedence over politics as a collective project based on social change. Even in social movements and critical thought today, we speak a lot about 'care'. Taking care of ourselves is the new revolution. This is perhaps one of today's key themes, from feminism to neighbourhood action, or local self-defence. But this care we talk about so much might be starting to look too much like palliative care.

This might be why the collective imagination of today is swarming with zombies, Dracula figures, and skulls. While we are becoming aware of this death that is already with us, we do not know how to respond to real death, to the old and ailing among us, to raped and murdered women, to refugees and immigrants who risk everything to cross borders. The posthumous condition is the afterwards of a death that is not our real death, but a historical death brought about by the prevailing narrative of our times. Why has this story triumphed so easily? It is evident that we are living, in real time, through a harshening of the material conditions of life, both economic and environmental. The limits of the planet and its resources are scientifically proven. The unsustainability of the economic system is also increasingly evident. But what is the source of this impotence that recruits us as such uncritical, docile agents of our own end? Why, if we are alive, do we accept a post-mortem scenario?

The Catastrophe of Time

In this posthumous condition, the relationship with death cuts through time in its three lived dimensions, thus submitting it to the experience of catastrophe. We are posthumous because, somehow, the irreversibility of our civilisational death belongs to an experience that already was. Walter Benjamin pondered a revolution that would simultaneously restore the unfulfilled promises of the future and the victims of the past. Revolution, seen from the theological scheme of salvation, would start time anew. The posthumous condition is the reverse of this revolution: endless death, damnation that is not going to come at the end of time, but rather becomes time-based. It is the catastrophe of time.

The 'catastrophe of time' is the expression Svetlana Alexievich uses to refer to Chernobyl. Her words, in fragments from the chapter titled 'The author interviews herself on missing history and why Chernobyl calls our view of the world into question' in *Chernobyl Prayer: Voices from Chernobyl* (Penguin, 2016) should be read directly and attentively.

> But I see Chernobyl as the beginning of a new history: it offers not only knowledge but also prescience, because it challenges our old ideas about ourselves and the world. When we talk about the past or the future, we read our ideas about time into those words; but Chernobyl is, above all, a catastrophe of time ...
>
> We were dazzled by infinity. The philosophers and writers fell silent, derailed from the familiar tracks of culture and tradition ...
>
> In the space of one night we shifted to another place in history. We took a leap into a new reality, and that reality proved beyond not only our knowledge but also our imagination. Time was out of joint. The past suddenly became impotent, it had nothing for us to draw on; in the all-encompassing – or so we'd believed – archive of humanity, we couldn't find a key to open this door ...
>
> What lingers most in my memory of Chernobyl is life afterwards: the possessions without owners, the landscapes without people. The roads going nowhere, the cables leading nowhere. You find yourself wondering just what this is: the past or the future ...
>
> [All] that is left of our knowledge is an awareness of how little we know ... Everything has changed, except us.

Chernobyl, Verdun, Auschwitz, Hiroshima, Nagasaki, Bhopal, Palestine, New York, South Africa, Iraq, Chechnya, Tijuana, Lesbos ... an endless geography of death that has devoured time and turned it into catastrophe. Massive death, administrated death, toxic death, atomic death. This is the induced death of millions of people, also bringing about the death of the subject, history, and the future of humanity. It is the death that postmodernity, with its celebration of the simulacrum in an interminable present, denied but that now returns with greater strength, which is indeed what happens with things that are repressed. Herein lies the weakness of postmodern culture, with everything it was also able to open up, for the eternal present of the simulacrum forgot about and denied death, even while speaking of it. It recognised finitude and fragility but not the death in dying or the death in killing. More specifically, it overlooked the difference between dying and being killed, between expiration and murder.

As Jean Baudrillard perceived, the simulacrum hid the crime, thus preventing us from thinking that the death we presently accept as a past and future horizon of our time is not that of our mortal condition, but that of our murderous vocation. It is crime. It is murder. This was understood by the Austrian writer Ingeborg Bachmann, author of an unfinished work and an unfinished life, who never confused human finitude with the social production of death, or 'death styles' (as she put it in *Todesarten*, the general title of her cycle of novels). Not for nothing had she studied philosophy and written her doctoral thesis, in the mid-1940s, challenging the figure of Heidegger and his philosophy of death. After abandoning philosophy as a discipline, Bachmann turned her attention to the word itself, stripped of all academicism, trusting in the possibility of still being able to find a true word. One of these true words, which changes the sense of the meaning of our time, is precisely 'murder'. She closes her unfinished novel *Malina* with this word. From the truth we are exposed to by this word, we might say, with Bachmann, that we are not becoming extinct but that we are being murdered, even though selectively. With this twist, with this break in the sense of our end, death is no longer projected onto the end of time but enters the present time, revealing the power relations that comprise it and which can be denounced and fought. The time of extinction is not the same as that of extermination, and neither is dying the same as killing.

In the fragment I just cited, Alexievich says that, of the past, only the wisdom of which we know nothing has been saved. In other words, it is the old Socratic condition of not knowing as a gateway to truer knowledge because it has passed through the depths of radical, critical questioning. Not-knowing, from this sovereign gesture of declaring oneself outside inherited sense, is the total opposite of illiteracy as social condemnation. It is a gesture of dissidence, of noncompliance with recognition and acceptance of the codes, messages, and arguments of power.

To declare our noncompliance with posthumous ideology is, in my view, the main task of critical thinking today. Any insubordination, unless of a suicidal or self-indulgent bent, needs tools for sustaining and sharing its position. In this case, we need conceptual, historical, poetic, and aesthetic instruments that can restore to us the personal and collective capacity to fight dogma and its political effects. I therefore propose an updating of the Enlightenment project, which is understood as a radical battle against credulousness. We have received the Enlightenment legacy through the catastrophe of the project of modernisation in which Europe colonised and shaped the world. Criticism of this project and its consequences must be constant and refined, today as well, working together with human and non-human cultures and forms of life, who suffered it as an invasion, as an imposition, both inside and outside of Europe. We must do this together because the modernisation agenda is putting at risk the very limits of the world we share. But this critique, precisely because it is a critique of the dogma of progress and its attendant forms of credulousness, takes us back to the roots of the Enlightenment as an attitude, not as a project, as a challenge to dogmas and the powers that benefit from them.

The Enlightenment storm is sparked precisely by the power of a wise not-knowing, to put it in Alexievich's terms. It is not scepticism but a battle of thought against establishment knowledge and its authorities, a battle of thought that trusts in the conviction that we can improve ourselves by thinking, and that only what contributes to that, one way or another, deserves to be thought. Rescuing this conviction does not mean going to the rescue of the future with which modernity sentenced the world to a non-future. On the contrary, it means starting to find the clues for weaving once again a time of the *liveable*. This conviction cannot be the monopoly of anyone, neither of a social class, nor of the intelligentsia, nor of certain social institutions, and nor of the European cultural identity. To be able to say, 'we do not believe you' is the most egalitarian expression of the common power of thought.

2

Enlightened Radicalism

I understand enlightenment as a battle against credulousness and its concomitant effects of domination. With the end of the seventeenth and early eighteenth centuries, the broad Enlightenment movement appeared in Europe. It was not defined by a common project but by a shared rejection of authoritarianism in its various forms (political, religious, moral, and so on). The fact that this movement crossed modern Europe does not mean, however, that enlightenment is a legacy linked to a European cultural identity or to a historical period, namely modernity. In fact, we could create a history of humanity by following and weaving together the threads of a number of enlightenments, many of them never heard or listened to, at different times and in different parts of the world. Hence we can wonder, today, about the possibility of a new radical enlightenment against the posthumous condition, an enlightenment that is neither modern nor postmodern, but already outside this cycle of lineal periodisation in the historical sense. A planetary enlightenment, perhaps, one more geographical than historical, and more of the world than universal.

In contrast to this definition of enlightenment, I understand modernisation as a specific historical project of the European ruling classes linked with industrial capitalism through colonisation. The modernisation of the world is a 'civilising' project that dualises reality in all its dimensions and hierarchises its value: old and new, past time and future time, tradition and innovation, the white race and others, technoscience and lesser knowledge, reason and superstition, use value and exchange value, us and them ... and, running through all of these oppositions, a basic duality that distinguishes between and places into direct opposition the natural world and the human world, nature and culture. In all these dualities, there is a positive sign and a negative sign, a plus and a minus. Of course, this entails a new operation of domination that affects all spheres of life, wherever modernisation has arrived. In recent decades, the wounds that this civilising project has left on our bodies and on our minds, on the planet's ecosystems, on languages, cultures, knowledge, and ways of life, throughout the world, has unleashed anger, a kind of antimodern consensus that includes, at the same time, a certain anti-enlightenment unanimity. Pankaj Mishra's book, *Age of Anger: A History of the Present* (Farrar, Straus and Giroux, 2017) captures a sanguinary cultural and political situation stemming from this resentment sown around the world by Western modernisation. Mishra makes a direct connection between the Enlightenment and modernisation as his main argument when describing the current catastrophe.

> The ambitious philosophers of the Enlightenment brought forth the idea of a perfectible society – a Heaven on Earth rather than in the afterlife. It was taken up vigorously by the French revolutionaries – Saint-Just, one of the most fanatical among them, memorably remarked, 'the idea of happiness is new in Europe' – before turning into the new political religions of the nineteenth century. Travelling deep into the postcolonial world in the twentieth century, it turned into a faith in top-down modernisation ...*

Confusion between the emancipatory impulse that guides the desire for a happy, dignified life on Earth, and the project of domination of all people and of all the world's natural

---

* Pankaj Mishra, *Age of Anger: A History of the Present*, New York: Farrar, Straus and Giroux, 2017, p. 156.

resources is dangerous, because doing so overlooks the inner combat against modernity itself and leaves us without references and without emancipatory tools with which to fight against the dogmatisms of our dark posthumous condition, its gurus and its saviours.

The distinction, internal to modernity, between the critical option of a radical, revolutionary enlightenment and the various moderate, reformist modern projects that redirect and neutralise it, has been explored by several historians who have altered the vision given to us by the front-runners of philosophy and modern politics. The best known among them is perhaps Jonathan Israel, but other leading figures like Margaret Jacob, Ann Thompson, Paul Hazard, and Philipp Blom have worked on similar lines before and afterwards. Thanks to them, more than through the history of philosophy, always written from the empire of Kant and German idealism, we can now gain access to another sense of the Enlightenment rupture and ask ourselves about its present relevance.

The fight against credulousness is not a wholesale attack on belief. Beliefs are necessary for life and for knowledge. Credulousness, on the other hand, is the basis of all domination because it entails delegation of intelligence and conviction. In the entry on 'Criticism' in the *Encyclopédie Française*, the authors say, 'Credulousness is the lot of the ignorant; determined incredulousness is that of the half-wise; methodical doubt is that of the wise.' For enlightenment, it is not a matter of establishing which knowledge is most correct but, rather, the most accurate relationship with each of the forms of experience and knowledge. This option does not, therefore, mean replacing religion with science and, as is often claimed, turning it into a new modern religion. Enlightenment is not a battle of science against religion or of reason against faith. This reductionist simplification distorts what is really at stake. What radical enlightenment demands is to be able to exercise the freedom to submit to scrutiny any knowledge and any belief, wherever it comes from and whoever formulates it, without presuppositions or arguments from authority. This necessary examination of the word of others and, in particular, of one's own thought, is what can then, in generic terms, be called criticism. Beyond the strict sense that this term had, referring to the work of interpretation of ancient texts, it came to mean, in the eighteenth century, according to the *Encyclopédie*, 'a clear examination and fair judgement of human productions'.

Criticism is not judgement from a position of superiority. On the contrary. It is the necessary attention demanded by reason which, knowing it is finite and uncertain, accepts its condition. The *Encyclopédie* continues, 'What, then must the critic do? ... In a word, convince the human spirit of its weakness so it can usefully employ the little strength it squanders in vain.' This is why Kant further radicalises the critical option. Not only do we need to submit to scrutiny the truths we produce (those of science, law, moral values, etc.) but reason itself should also be subjected to its own criticism, suspect itself, and always interrogate itself as to its desires and limits. As Goya pointed out, 'reason produces monsters' – but Kant himself could have written the same.

From an enlightenment point of view, criticism is therefore self-criticism, scrutiny is self-scrutiny, education is self-education. In short, criticism is autonomy of thought but not self-sufficiency of reason. The guiding question of enlightenment is not, then, the 'how long?' of the posthumous condition but the 'how far?' of criticism. How far can we explore nature without going astray or destroying it? How far can we ask ourselves about principles and fundamentals without prejudice? How far and for whom are certain moral values – and certain gods – valid? How far do we want to be governed under certain laws and by certain sovereigns? Criticism is an art of limits that restores our autonomy and sovereignty.

Reason is autonomous but not self-sufficient, because enlightenment dares to accept the natural character of the human condition. In continuity with nature but not beyond it, the human spirit cannot aspire to a privileged vision, or to superior intelligibility, or an eternal truth. Knowledge means work, developing, trial and error, continuous, unfinished elaboration of the meaning and value of human experience. At the roots of the Enlightenment, before its idealist and positivist apprehension, there is a re-encounter with the bodily and carnal condition of the human being. Ancient materialism, that of Democritus, Epicurus, and Lucretius, taken through covert readings of Spinoza, enters the scene once again. How can one argue that matter thinks, and what are the consequences of this assertion? This is the question that radical enlightenment leaves us with, through the deliberations of authors like Diderot, Baron d'Holbach, John Toland, Helvétius, Voltaire, Rousseau, Pierre Bayle, Hobbes, and La Mettrie. It is no longer a matter of the word becoming flesh, but that flesh produces words, and the words have consequences in the ways we are going to live in our flesh.

Embracing the natural and bodily condition of the human means accepting the incompleteness and precariousness of our truths, but also the perfectibility of what we are and what we make of ourselves. To know no longer means gaining access to God's eternal truths but improving our own understanding and relationship with the world around us. The men of the Enlightenment were not deluded by progress. Later disenchantment has all too often portrayed them as such, gullible in the self-same credulousness they were fighting against. Radical enlightenment is not deluded but combative. And its commitment, from Spinoza to Marx, and even including Nietzsche, is none other than improvement of the human species, and fighting against everything that routinely oppresses and degrades it. Throughout the eighteenth century, direct experience of material prosperity, especially in industrial and colonial England, would profoundly alter the meaning of this moral, political, and scientific demand to 'improve ourselves' through knowledge. 'To improve' gradually came to mean to prosper, and humanity's progress thus came to be identified with increased wealth. This distortion by political economy of the meaning of emancipation is one of the great shifts that would neutralise the radical nature of the critical project of the Enlightenment. The other was to come from more internal forces, from the public sphere itself, as a new form of servitude: cultural servitude.

Cultural Servitude

With the consolidation of the modern state and its forms of power, the public sphere was constituted as a system of culture. The dissolution of theocratic power and the old social hierarchy made of culture the principal means by which to give form and meaning to collective life, its relations of belonging, and its mechanisms of enforcing obedience. In contrast with bonds of obligation (religious, lineage, and vassalage), the system of culture is responsible for moulding freely conforming citizens. At the same time, it must make clear both their autonomy as subjects and their compliance as citizens. In the modern state, the contract is the form this bond takes: the social contract and the labour contract. And this contract presupposes, albeit formally, the free consent of the parties. How can free consent be guided? Why with some and not with others? How far do the demands of mutual involvement extend? Modern culture mobilises two ideas, national identity and economic prosperity, as its main arguments for free association. This is the form of what La Boétie had already analysed in the sixteenth century, namely voluntary servitude now deployed as cultural servitude.

Hegel, the philosopher who brought together the concept of the self-cultivation (*Bildung*) of humanity and its culmination in the form of the state, gives a clear explanation of how the culture system works in this project of free subordination. He writes in *Elements of the Philosophy of Right,*

> *Education,* in its absolute determination, is therefore *liberation* and *work* towards a higher liberation ... [This] liberation is the *hard work* of opposing mere subjectivity of conduct, of opposing the immediacy of desire as well as the subjective vanity of feeling [*Empfindung*] and the arbitrariness of caprice. The fact that it is such hard work accounts for some of the disfavour which it incurs.*

What culture does, therefore, is to free citizens from particularisms in order to integrate the subject into the state; freeing them from immediacy to force them into arbitration; emancipating them from arbitrariness to awaken them to the point of view of universality. Emancipation and subjugation, freedom and obedience meet in seamless coexistence. Autonomy has been reshaped into willing obedience. A few decades later, Freud in his *Civilisation and Its Discontents* would analyse the pain of this repressive, enforced integration and its psychic and political essence.

In opposition to this cultural servitude, radical criticism and its battle against credulousness and its forms of oppression becomes criticism of culture, by which I mean an unmasking of culture as a system of political subjugation. This criticism is not one that emanates from the gaze of an external, impervious judge but from a self-diagnosis of the body and suffering minds suppressed by the project of culture and its political responsibility. Nietzsche unmasks the values of a resentful, unhealthy morality in the European culture of his day. Romanticism exposes the silenced alienation in the successes of modernisation. Marx shows how the class interests of the bourgeoisie are accommodated within it, and how they work. Feminism reveals

---

* G. W. F. Hegel, *Elements of the Philosophy of Right*, ed. Allen W. Wood, trans. H. B. Nisbet, Cambridge: Cambridge University Press, 1991, p. 225.

the productive and reproductive political discrimination that is concealed beneath the discourse of universal emancipation. Walter Benjamin pointed out the rest, this part that is missing from narratives of progress, even revolutionary ones. The critical theory of his Frankfurt School colleagues denounces the violence of the culture industry and its destructive effects. The various schools of postcolonial thought establish the intrinsic relationship between colonialism and modernity.

And so it goes, up to the present day, when the global institutions of culture have become the permanent headquarters of cultural criticism. This is especially so with museums of contemporary art, but also with cultural studies, faculties of philosophy and the human sciences, as well as a good number of essays on contemporary thought. The problem is that, when culture is reduced to criticism of culture, its autonomy is condemned to self-referentiality: philosophy as criticism of philosophy, art as criticism of the art institution, literature as criticism of literary forms, and so on. This circularity is part of our posthumous experience, since it is an exercise of criticism that can only move in the space that remains between what there was and the impossibility of being something else. Like a closed water loop, it appears to move but goes nowhere as it rots. We must get out of this loop and situate the need for criticism at its roots. Denouncing the relations between knowledge and power is of no intrinsic interest and only acquires value in its emancipatory effects or, in other words, to the extent that it gives us back the ability to explore the meaning and value of human experience from a standpoint of an affirmation of its freedom and dignity.

In fact, the first Enlightenment thinkers warned of this danger. Far from ingenuously believing that science and education would, in themselves, deliver the human species from obscurantism and oppression, what they proposed was the need to examine which knowledge and which education would contribute to emancipation, while regarding any salvation-minded temptation as suspect. Many readings of Rousseau's *Discourse on the Arts and Sciences*, and Diderot's *Rameau's Nephew*, among other texts, are required if one is not to simplify the magnitude of the Enlightenment challenge. From their initial friendship and their subsequent distancing, Diderot and Rousseau were fully aware that the culture of their time was the main cover for a hypocritical and toadying system of power that, by displacing earlier power relations, kept reproducing them. In his *Discourse*, Rousseau wrote, 'Suspicions, offences, fears, coldness, reserve, hatred, and betrayal will always be hiding under this uniform and perfidious veil of politeness, under that urbanity which is so praised and which we owe to our century's enlightenment.' But it was not only the disenchanted, reclusive, pre-Romantic Rousseau who understood these things, because Diderot, '*le philosophe*', also shows the limits of enlightened dogma when Rameau, the down-and-out relative of the great musician of the day, is dismissed by his masters with the following words: 'I do believe it thinks it can have sense and reason! Out! We have got quite enough of those things ourselves.' Diderot's *Rameau's Nephew* thus portrays with this behaviour the stance of a ruling class that is starting to monopolise and instrumentalise access to culture and knowledge.

Both men glimpsed the cultural servitude that the Enlightenment was beginning to foster. Both denounced the simulacrum and warned against any form of culturally minded naivety. With the enlightened venture, its own critique was born and, with self-confidence, suspicion. This is an essentially Enlightenment position, in which self-criticism is not confused with self-referentiality. This implacable relationship between the Enlightenment venture and criticism of its own dangers is what we need to update today. The problem is that they have been separated. On the one hand, exploitation of disenchantment with the destructive effects of modernisation and its fraudulence when it comes to building fairer and freer societies increasingly reinforces the anti-enlightenment crusade. On the other hand, faced with the catastrophe of our time and invoking their power to save us, we demand more knowledge and more education. It is like a mantra, repeated again and again, though it is hardly supported by any demonstrable argument. The decisive fact of our time is that, on the whole, we know a lot and yet we can do very little. We are both enlightened and illiterate.

Rousseau decried the uncoupling of cultural development and moral development. Diderot demonstrated the relations of economic domination that underpinned the simulacrum of morality and aesthetic sensibility in the enlightened society. That split today is even more radical. We know everything and can do nothing. There is no need for any simulacrum. Our science and our ignorance are brazenly joined at the hip. We are living in times of enlightened ignorance.

Enlightened Illiteracy

A new problem arises with the battle against credulousness. Having access to the available knowledge of our time is not sufficient. What is important is being able to relate to it in such a way that it contributes to our changing ourselves and our world for the better. If we potentially know everything but can do nothing, what is the point of this knowledge? We fall into the same trap of uselessness, redundancy, and disorientation that the Enlightenment denounced: over-informed credulousness. We must therefore go beyond the struggle for free access to knowledge, which is the necessary but not sufficient condition of emancipation.

In fact, the problem of universal access to knowledge is a modern concern. With increased scientific, artistic, and media production, the question about who can have access to what comes to the fore. Conversely, in ancient Greece and many other cultures, the main problem was not access to knowledge but the understanding of truth and its effects on life. This is confirmed by fragments from Heraclitus, the Platonic dialogues, and Taoist texts like the *Laozi* or the *Zhuangzi*. What is the point of knowing this or that if we are a long way from understanding its meaning? *Logos*, the idea, Tao ... the names change to signify the same thing: knowledge is not specific information or discourse but a way of relating ourselves with being, the being of the world around us, and our own being. That is, if they can be separated. The problem of access, then, is not one of availability but one of the path, an approach that entails displacement. When, in the West, monotheism incorporates its religious matrix into the Greek philosophical and scientific substratum, the idea is retained but the path of truth implies the condition that it has been revealed and is sustained through faith. But the fact remains the same: the relationship with truth meaningfully changes our position and our way of being in the world. It is understanding or, in more religious terms, illumination or revelation.

With the scientific revolution, which, between the sixteenth and eighteenth centuries in Europe, was experienced as a blooming of new experimental data and techniques, and the knowledge being constructed as a result, the problem of access began to have the meaning we give to it today. Who and which institutions must be responsible for, and have the monopoly of, this knowledge? How is it to be communicated and stored? Who should be its audiences, recipients, spokespersons, and beneficiaries? It was not long before manuals, dictionaries, and encyclopaedias became coveted bestsellers, or before associations and academies of science were emancipated from the political and religious institutions that had hitherto been the custodians of knowledge, or before the public sphere began to be nourished by what we might now call scientific production, by means of printed publications of continually increasing circulation. It was then that pedagogical and political questions arose about the universalisation of state or public education in European countries and, to some extent, in their colonies. Access to education for everyone then became – and has been, through to the present day – one of the main points of any emancipatory political programme that is guided by notions of equality, freedom, and justice.

However, by then, these same leaders of the Enlightenment movement had found that the availability and accessibility of new knowledge, produced in ever greater quantities and at ever greater speed, did not solve the problem but, rather, gave rise to new ones. Under the heading of 'Criticism' in the *Encyclopédie*, the authors pointed out the inevitability of this because of problems that look contemporary to us, namely, speed, arbitrariness, uselessness, and the inability to digest, or understand, what is being produced.

> The desire to know is often sterile because of an excess of activity. Truth needs to be looked for, but it must also be waited for, gone ahead of, but never beyond. The critic is the wise guide who must oblige the traveller to stop when the day ends, before getting lost in the darkness.
>
> ... Discoveries require a time of maturation before which inquiries seem to be fruitless. A truth waits to bloom, for the coming together of its elements ... Critics must carefully observe this fermentation of the human spirit, this digestion of our knowledge ... They would thereby succeed in imposing silence on those who only swell the volume of science without increasing its treasure ... We would then free so much space in our libraries! All these authors who jabber on about science instead of reasoning would be removed from the list of useful books. Then we would have much less to read and much more to glean.

Even then, in the middle of the eighteenth century, it was feared that libraries would be saturated, that useless data would accumulate, and that it would be impossible to relate adequately to knowledge. Without the practice of criticism, knowledge tends to become useless because, although we might have access to its contents, we do not know how or from where to relate to them. Criticism, as the *Encyclopédie* describes, takes place in a whole set of activities, including selecting, checking, verifying, discarding, relating, and putting in context, among others. It not only confirms but validates, not only accumulates but questions, meaning, both dynamically and contextually. We are not so far removed from this situation, although conditions have changed and become much more complex.

Nowadays, we have few restrictions on access to knowledge but there are numerous mechanisms for neutralising criticism. Among many others, four are outstanding: saturation of attention; segmentation of audiences; standardisation of languages; and the hegemony of solutionism.

Neutralising Criticism

The encyclopaedists referred to the slow pace of truth and the difficulty of digesting available knowledge. If they had imagined for a moment the magnitude of the problem two and a half centuries later, they would surely have succumbed to incurable indigestion. The leap has been exponential, in terms of both speed and quantity. Today, we have statistics on publication, scientific production, and the datification of collective activity that are close to science fiction magnitudes. Related to this phenomenon are two notions that have become relevant in recent years: economy of attention and interpassivity.

The former term, coined by the economist Michael Goldhaber, refers to the fact that when the volume of information we relate to increases so much, the problem is no longer just the need to select it but also the impossibility of paying attention to it all. How can we select if we cannot be attentive to everything around us? How can we discriminate critically if we cannot process (digest) everything? It is obvious that the exponential growth of information and of knowledge means that a good part of it all remains disregarded and, therefore, what then becomes a scarce and valuable asset is not information but attention itself.

This is the conclusion in terms of economy of attention but, in addition to that, we need to develop a psychology and a politics of attention. The former is related to the pathologies caused by the saturation of attention itself: anxiety, disorientation, and depression. The latter pertains to the consequences and political challenges arising from this saturation of attention, which are basically impotence and dependence. We cannot have opinions, especially about what is happening around us. The twofold limit of attention – reception of data and information and their processing in the form of opinions and knowledge – results in paralysis in the face of an overwhelming scenario. Overwhelming subjectivity is what most easily submits to acritical agreement with the opinions, ideology, and judgements of others. Since we cannot form an opinion about everything around us, we follow or subscribe to the already packaged views that others offer us, without being able to submit them to criticism. Is not this the mechanism of what Kant called heteronomy? The difference is that, in other times, heteronomy was based on ignorance as an absence of knowledge, as non-access to knowledge, while, today, it is underpinned by overwhelming, and hence inoperative, accessibility.

Every epoch and every society has its own forms of ignorance, each giving rise to its concomitant forms of credulousness. Ours is an ignorance drowning in knowledge that cannot be digested or processed. One of its more extreme forms has been called 'interpassivity' or 'interpassive subjectivity', terms that were coined by the Viennese philosopher Robert Pfaller and taken up as well, on more than one occasion, by the culture critic Slavov Žižek. Interpassivity is a form of delegated activity that conceals passivity or, more specifically, it resides in everything we do not do, letting someone else, usually a machine, do it for us, from the photocopies we have made but never get round to reading (as Umberto Eco pointed out, referring to academics) to the songs and films we download but never listen to or watch. The machine's done it for us. It is a relationship without relationship, one which moves information but, obviously, fails to generate experience, understanding, or any shift at all.

Warnings about the dangers of specialisation have been around for a long time. Development of the sciences and techniques of modernity led to a progressive difficulty in and autonomisation among the various disciplines, and with respect to the common trunk of philosophy. The result was the appearance of a new kind of ignorance that inevitably affects all of us today: that of knowing about only one discipline and utterly ignoring the most basic notions of the rest. This tendency was cushioned until the middle of the twentieth century with the idea of general culture, which worked as a container and sounding board for the experiences offered by the different scientific, artistic, and humanistic specialties, albeit in a highly simplified form. Nowadays, even this idea has become impracticable.

The question that then arises is: have we all become specialists and only specialists? The answer is: this is not the case either. True specialisation, ever more complex and demanding, remains in the hands of very few people, while what is generally produced is a segmentation of knowledge and audiences. This occurs in both the market and in academia. We are offered knowledge and technological and cultural products in accordance with segmentation by age, income, origins, and so on.

The segment is not a fragment. In discussions about postmodernity, there was much more talk about the value of the fragment when great narratives were ending. The fragment was ambivalent, at once ruinous and free. Something broken and something liberated that opened up a field of uncertainty and the possibility of new relationships. The segment, however, is an elaboration that categorises, guides, and organises the reception of knowledge. It establishes the distance for managing it in a way that is predictable and identifiable.

Segmentation of knowledge and its audiences is related, rather, to a standardisation of cognitive production. What seems distant in terms of content becomes similar in terms of procedures. Transversality no longer links up experiences but modes of functioning. Whatever it is about, the point is that everything works the same way. Three examples of this are academic activity, the world of fashion, and the media opinion-forming apparatus. In all three cases, we see a similar situation, which is to say, a juxtaposition of contents that function according to the same parameters and protocols. In the case of academia, sciences that do not communicate among themselves are taught and researched with the same temporal parameters, from the same institutional devices, and in keeping with the same criteria of evaluation. In the university, we do not even understand what our colleagues in the same department are talking about, but what is guaranteed is that all of us, in all the universities around the world, know how to function in the same way.

The same thing happens with fashion: the same timetables, seasons, acceleration of changes, and personalisation of trends which, however, are all made to move in unison through the same streets of the same cities depending on the intensity of demand and according to an identical need for incessantly changing appearances so that nothing changes. As for the domain of opinion, which now dominates, minute by minute, the common sense of the whole population through the media, we see the same standardisation of what is thinkable, taken to the point of paroxysm. Opinions are offered, one after another, with more or less staging of the conflict between them depending on audiences, but always with the same underlying assumption, which is that the fact of having an opinion cancels out the need of having to go one step further so that the matter can be questioned. All opinions have the same value because that is what they are: opinions. Standardised as such, they are stripped of all powers of challenging and questioning. They are expressed side by side but have lost all possibility of communicating with each other. Segmentation and standardisation are two processes that, paradoxically, advance hand in hand with the result of orderly, predictable management of non-communication among forms of knowledge and of their reciprocal uselessness.

Delegated Intelligence

This idea of the management of knowledge and its results is what feeds solutionist ideology, which is presently becoming hegemonic. As Evgeny Morozov and others define it, solution-ism is the ideology that legitimates and endorses the aspiration of approaching any complex social situation by means of clear definition and definitive solutions. With origins in the domain of urban planning and ideologically developed in Silicon Valley, the term 'solutionism' has its own utopia, that of transporting humanity to a world without problems. In this problem-free world, human beings can be stupid because the world itself, with all the objects, devices, and data that shape it, and the operations that organise it, will be intelligent. In the solution-ist utopia, the plan is no longer to increase productive power to expand human capacities but to delegate intelligence itself, in an unprecedented move of anthropological pessimism. Let them, the machines, decide because we humans have not only become too small, as Günther Anders affirmed, but we always end up causing problems as well. Artificial intelligence, thus understood, is delegated intelligence. What is worrying about this is not that it is exercised by a machine, a bacterium, a par-ticle, or whatever device, but that this is deemed unproblematic and is therefore unreflective. It can learn and correct itself by accumulating data. Self-education now means self-correction. Yet it cannot engage in self-examination or submit itself to fair scrutiny because it is non-problematic, acritical. Stupid humans in an intelligent world. This is the perfect utopia.

The credulousness of our times leads to a two-sided dogma, which is to say, apocalypse or solutionism; either the irreversibility of destruction, including extinction, or the unquestionability of technical solutions, which we are never equipped to discover. If we have been left without a future, it is because the relationship with what could happen has been totally disconnected from what we can do. That is why it does not matter if we know. We can know everything, as I was saying, but we still cannot do anything with this knowledge. Even today's education, with its renovating discourse and projects, preaches this disconnection. We must prepare ourselves for a future we know nothing about. There is no more despotic and terrifying statement than this. This is not openness to uncertainty and creativity but a disconnection between action and present learning with respect to future consequences. Deresponsibilisation and depoliticisation are the conditions for the delegation of intelligence. It means the rupture of the ethical nexus of action. The forms of oppression that come with this credulousness are very diverse, from new forms of material inequality and cultural extremes through to phenomena of the degradation of life in all its physical and mental aspects, degradation of the poor, and degradation of elites who do not even know whether or not they are running the world that is fast enriching them. With all their diversity of forms, all the varieties of oppression in our time entail acceptance of a 'we do not know how to think about what is happening or how to intervene in it'.

Given this deactivation of critical subjectivity, the main challenge faced by a new radical enlightenment is to return to the centre of any debate the status of the human and its place in the world, and in relation with non-human forms of existence.

This is not a matter of prolonging the unfinished project of modernity, as Habermas suggested in the 1980s, because it is not a task of the past but about a war that is being waged against our future. Adorno and Horkheimer painfully observed in 1947 that the marriage between humans and nature was a story that, with the Enlightenment, had ended badly. And they were right, if the only possible story of this marriage was that written by capitalist, Eurocentric, and anthropocentric modernisation. In the current planetary era, the match between man and nature is no longer patriarchal marriage, with all its dangers and structures of domination, but something that is rather more uncertain. What remains to be resolved seems to be – only – who will destroy whom. In this situation, the utopia of delegated intelligence is preparing for a new conception of survival that is neither natural nor human but post-human, post-natural, or simply posthumous.

There is a question, however, that no form of solutionist dogmatism can resolve, the one that, in the sixteenth century, La Boétie considered to be at the root of all refusal to accept voluntary servitude. Is this living? As he wrote it, this is a question that is within the reach of anybody and that can appear in any context of life. It does not appeal to a calculable objectivity but to a dignity that can always be called into question. In brief, it is a question that can be shared but not delegated, because what it expresses is that life consists in producing the sense and conditions of the *liveable*. Returning to this question today and pitting it against the forms of credulousness and servitude of our time means affirming that humanity's time might be running out but that the human is precisely what is not coming to an end. To reappropriate this unfinishedness is to reappropriate our condition and our reflexive intelligence without breaking with the continuum of non-human intelligences, while also not submitting them to our dictates. From this standpoint, the humanities are not a set of disciplines in danger of extinction but a battlefield in which the sense and value of human experience are determined. It is not a matter of defending them but, rather, of engaging forcefully with what, through them, is at stake. It means confronting the humanities in danger of extinction with the humanities in transition.

3

Humanities in Transition

I borrow the term 'in transition' from the Transition Towns ecology movement which, in response to the environmental crisis, suggests specific measures and life choices that encourage a paradigm shift in our cities. With the idea of 'in transition', acknowledgement of the crisis is directly linked with the possibility of criticism and to the present time of transformation. Talking about transition may sweeten the reality and make us see what is not there, but what is relevant is the change of perspective. In other words, instead of thinking about what we are losing and what we must preserve, or what future models we must dream of, it focuses on what is happening, what we are doing, and, therefore, also on what we can do, here and now.

By 'humanities' we can no longer refer only to the theoretical disciplines of 'Letters' but must also include all the activities (sciences, arts, crafts, techniques, creative practices ...) with which we process the sense of human experience and affirm its dignity and freedom. We are no longer guided by the divisions between science and letters, theory and practice, academic knowledge and informal knowledge. We need to understand what we are doing on the basis of shared problems that move through different languages, practices, and capacities.

As in the case of ecologism, debates about the so-called crisis of the humanities have stayed trapped in the narrow space between two poles. On the one hand, there is lament and alarm about what is being lost, and calls for preservation (of a legacy, traditions, habits, and even of their supposed ethical and political virtues). On the other hand are designs for the future, often linked with technological utopianism and the cognitive salvation of humanity thanks to the connectedness of all our knowledge in the global hypertext. Both positions, the defensive-nostalgic and the techno-utopian, remove us from present reality and our challenges and commitments. In order to come closer to this reality, I suggest reflection by way of five hypotheses.

Hypothesis 1. What we perceive as disinterest is, in fact, a deinstitutionalisation of humanistic activities by the cognitive project of present-day capitalism.

There is a tendency among nostalgic humanists to warn of and lament the lack of interest by the market, and among people in general, in everything that has no immediate utility or benefit. To begin with, two things must be said in this regard. First, many people have not lost interest in understanding and making sense of their personal and collective experience. Second, today's capitalism has not given up its interest in knowledge, education, and culture but, on the contrary, has placed them at the centre of a crystal-clear epistemological project with very definite objectives.

The epistemological project of capitalism today is connected with what, some years ago, was called the 'fourth scientific and industrial revolution', which goes beyond digitalisation in the knowledge and information society. Whether it is real or not, or only an ideological effect of a technological shift, what is relevant is that we are moving into a paradigm of innovation that exceeds what is entailed by this digitalisation. As I understand it, the most important aspect of the fourth revolution is that its aim is the development of intelligence above and beyond human consciousness (the internet of things, intelligent manufacturing, genetic design, big data), placing in continuity the biological, physical, and digital worlds. Hence, we are not

looking at a mere commodification of knowledge but at the pri-
oritising of certain kinds of skills and intelligence, which also
very directly include multiple and emotional intelligences. This
is a revolution that does not depend on one scientific language
alone but that mobilises all the kinds of knowledge available to
us in the service of a single aim, which is to make of intelligence
as such something that is above and beyond the human being,
as a productive force. I'm referring to an intelligence that is
more and less than human. Where does this leave intelligence,
then, as an autonomous, reflective power?

The capitalist educational project that is presently underway
is situated in this epistemological framework. The school of
the future is already being constructed, and its constructors
are not thinking about states or communities but about big
communication companies and banks. It has no walls or fences
but, instead, online platforms and teachers twenty-four hours
a day. There will be no need for it to be exclusionary because
it will individualise talents, life histories, and learning paths. It
will practise universality without equality, an idea that we will
need to start thinking about because, if it is not already so, it
will be the educational condition of our time.

In the framework of this global epistemological educational
project, the deinstitutionalisation of the humanities has many
aspects. I will detail some of the most significant among them.
First, the change of direction in the public system which, from
being based on the cultural and political project of the nation-
state is now being conceived as a promotional element of the
competitive market of talents, skills, and patents. This move
depoliticises cultural policies, and departments and ministries
are being taken over by promotors, consultants, business
groups, think-tanks, and so on. And these are the people who
set the agenda for the administrations.

Second, there is a progressive detaching of the workforce
through precaritisation. The new employment conditions in
the educational, academic, and cultural sectors result in the fact

that nobody 'belongs' to the institution, company, or project where they work, and neither is there any process of sustainable co-involvement among colleagues. Moreover, economic dualisation is a combination of ever greater oligarchies and precariat. Some examples are researchers with high-profile contracts, together with broad ranks of non-tenured lecturers in the universities, journalists with extremely high salaries working with teams of scholarship holders, and so forth. At the extremes of this phenomenon, we also find direct demonetarisation of 'redundant' activities or of those that do not fit with the new epistemological and cultural regime. These are the ones that end up being done without remuneration not because non-payment is desired but because that is the condition for them to happen.

Third, also contributing to the deinstitutionalisation of the humanities are active desertions from academia and the structural overburdening caused by this process. Good students leave the university or rule out an academic career because it does not make sense. Researchers forsake their studies because they cannot stand the workaday, affective, and human humiliations they entail. Artists flee from the projects market and its competitive calls for entries and look for ways to share their work by means of other channels. Teachers opt for alternative educational projects. And so on. Desertions and overburdening are generating new forms of self-organisation and funding, but they are also reinforcing the tendency to segmentation, disintegration, the shaping of microworlds, and self-referencing because each element is circumscribed to smaller, increasingly identity-based communities.

This raises questions. Is this trend of deinstitutionalisation favourable or unfavourable? What does it restrict and what does it permit? Must we hope for new forms of institutionality or recover the traditional institutions in keeping with other logics? What does the dissemination of intellectuality free us from and what does its precaritisation condemn us to? In this ambivalent terrain of deinstitutionalisation that fragments and expels while, at the same time, empowering critical and crea-tive processes, what can be observed, among other things, is the increasing dissociation of humanistic activities from a col-lective project of emancipation that would be able to respond adequately to the project of cognitive capitalism. And hence the need for my second hypothesis.

Hypothesis 2. Right now, we know more about the relationship between knowledge and power than about the relationship between knowledge and emancipation.

If the humanities are concerned with the ability freely to form and give sense to human experience and dignity, we must understand that their crisis is directly related to the distance that has opened up between what we know about the world and ourselves, and our ability to transform our conditions of life. We have seen that, historically speaking, knowing more, having more education, getting more information, and so on, does not make us freer or ethically better. Neither has this contributed towards creating more emancipated societies and hence the deep disproportion that assails us and turns us into enlightened illiterates.

Foucault, following the line of open criticism taken up by others, including Nietzsche, taught us to see that, behind the Enlightenment promise of emancipation through science and education, new power relations were being organised: power over bodies, over codes of language, over habits and behaviour, over institutional structures, over national projects, and so on. Every form of knowledge entails power relations. This idea has become for us an unquestionable premise, almost a truism. On this basis, we can, and often do, analyse the power relations that are inscribed in the knowledge of our time. We have very sophisticated tools for criticising and examining the effects of control over knowledge, its applications, and its transmission.

However, at the same time, when we defend the ethical and

political virtues of knowledge and education, their need for democracy and justice, we frequently fall back on such trite arguments that not even the enlightened ones of the eighteenth century fell for, because they already suspected the existence of their dark spots and perversities. As we have seen, even then, they were wary of culture if it did not come with criticism and self-criticism.

In Ettore Scola's film *Una giornata particolare*, Antonietta says, 'You can do anything to an uneducated woman.' What we must ask today is how and why so many educated people can have anything done to them. And why so many apparently cultured societies continue to commit so many atrocities. These are questions that were being asked in critical theory well into the twentieth century when the failure of culture was proclaimed. Not only did enlightened Europe fail to prevent fascism and war, but critical and revolutionary (anarchism, socialism, communism ...) thought did not, in practice, lead to more emancipated societies.

The main problem, then, is to redefine the meanings of emancipation and its relationship with the forms of knowledge of our time. What kinds of knowledge and what cultural practices do we need to construct, develop, and share to work for a better society throughout the planet? It seems a naïve question, but when the humanities lose touch with it, they become mere knowledge of texts about texts, and die. Redefining the meanings of emancipation is what humanistic activities must be about if they want to be rather more than a set of disciplines that are past their use-by date.

Hypothesis 3. The Western humanist tradition must abandon expansive universalism and learn to think from a standpoint of reciprocal universalism.

Humanism is a form of imperialism, a Eurocentric and patriarchal imperialism. Humanism, as a conception of man coming from the human sciences and political institutions of modernity, is based on the notion that the white, bourgeois, European male has of himself and is hegemonically imposed on any other conception of what is human, inside and outside of Europe.

This thesis seems to be well accepted in the domain of academic critical thought, especially in countries with a colonial past. There is also a rich, indispensable range of criticisms of humanism from gender, race, culture, political, economic relations, and other points of view, which have revealed the imperialist and patriarchal nature of humanism. They range from twentieth-century philosophical antihumanism (Heidegger, Foucault, poststructuralism, and so on) through to the various kinds of posthumanism, from postcolonial and decolonial studies to gender thought in its different branches and positions.

Yet at the same time, we have taken criticism of the humanist discipline and ideology so far that, for years, the human arts and sciences have tended to become a criticism of themselves, their assumptions, and the effects of subjugation. As a result, humanistic studies have been adopting either a defensive position or one of constraint and regret. Neither stance is interesting and, paradoxically, they are both essentially closed and self-referential.

The question we need to ask today must take us beyond criticism and denial. If humanism is a form of imperialism, can it cease to be so? And what would happen if it stopped being that? Or should we do what techno-capitalism and the fourth industrial revolution have already started, and just get rid of it altogether?

It is interesting to see how feminist philosophers like Judith Butler and Rosi Braidotti, who can hardly be suspected of Eurocentrism, are rescuing the possibility of calling for a certain legacy of humanism, in spite of everything. This is not any nostalgic or essentialist advocacy but, on the contrary, they are opening up the possibility of a mutinous option of not surrendering our lives to a capitalist management of intelligence, of connections, and emotions, and not letting ourselves become a physical-psychic asset of present-day necro-capitalism.

I think they are both pointing out that criticism of historical humanism and its universal models must not eliminate in us the ability to link ourselves to the common pool of human experience. For me, the common pool of human experience does not refer to a model, and neither is it Vitruvian Man or any other abstraction. It is not the cultural corpus of dead white men either. It is the ability we have to share basic experiences of life, like death, love, commitment, fear, the sense of dignity and justice, caring, and so on. What avenues do we have for exploring those proximities and for constructing a meaning of human experience without projecting one model onto another? Rather than being rejected, humanism and the European cultural legacy as a whole need to be put in their place, one place among others in the shared destiny of humanity. It is not about staying with the idea of a juxtaposition of cultures, which has already been exhausted by the multicultural model as a way of neutralising diversity with its tensions and reciprocities but, rather, about occupying a receptive and listening position that includes not only cultural otherness but also the tensions and antagonisms of ways of life inside and outside of Europe. This means criticising and also leaving behind both expansive universalism and defensive particularism in order to learn how to construct reciprocal universalisms or, as Merleau-Ponty put it, lateral universals, which is to say those that do not come from above but are constructed through crosswise relations, and horizontality.

Hypothesis 4. In the shared destiny of humanity, the most relevant epistemological fact of our present is the rediscovery of the nature–culture continuity.

In many of its expressions, contemporary culture has once again placed at its centre the natural condition of the human being as a species, and that of the subject as an incarnated subject. Contemporary critical culture is reinterpreting this fact – one that in other cultures has always been accepted – and the project of cognitive capitalism also understands it and is exploiting it, as I have described. Hence, the question is: are we able to propose and construct other meanings of this nature–culture re-encounter that are not subjected to present-day capitalism's patterns of exploitation? As I see it, this question locates the starting point from which the humanities can begin to redefine, today, the meanings of emancipation.

As Klaus Schwab, one of the promotors of the fourth scientific and industrial revolution, explained in a presentation at the 2016 World Economic Forum in Davos ('Mastering the Fourth Industrial Revolution'), the challenge now is to develop a whole gamut of new technologies that will merge the physical, digital, and biological realms in such a way that all disciplines, economies, and industries are involved. In some of his public declarations, Schwab says that this perspective even challenges ideas of what it means to be human. This challenge raises many questions, and they are not the same for everyone. From the standpoint of capitalism, the question is selective: who will be equipped to ride the wave of this fourth revolution? Which countries, which institutions, which companies, and which people, selected individually according to their talents? And which ones will be excluded and reduced to brute strength or human surplus?

From the ethical and political perspectives, however, what is at stake is the very meaning of human dignity and freedom in their condition of reciprocal universals to be worked out in a shared way. For the humanist Pico della Mirandola, in his *Oration on the Dignity of Man*, being able to ask about our dignity openly and in a way that is not predetermined was what made us human. *Dignitas* was not one attribute or another but the very possibility of being able to ponder what the status of human experience is from the perspective of improving its condition.

From this point of view, the re-encounter of nature and culture, the given and the constructed, or humanity as a species and as an idea, does not have only one meaning or only one plan for making it happen. Quite the contrary. The fact that the humanities are presently in transition shows that the meaning of what is human is in dispute. This is no idle or gratuitous quarrel because the interests of everyone against the interests of present-day capitalism are at stake. It does not arise, then, from a battle between non-profit and profit, as Martha Nussbaum asserts in her defence of the humanities. Neither does it come from the tension between the useless and usefulness, as Nuccio Ordine argues in his famous essay on the matter. These remain idealist positions typical of a bourgeoisie that could still distinguish between what fed the stomach and what fed the spirit. Today, the precariat of culture, the humanities, and academia cannot and does not want to make this distinction. Still less able to do so are the millions of people whose lives are presently at the limits of the *unliveable*. Our stomach, our conscience, and the dignity of humanity's shared destiny are at stake in the time that is left to us. Today, our battle is one of what is necessary against what is presented to us as imperative.

Hypothesis 5. We have lost the future, but we cannot keep wasting time.

One of the basic elements of this crisis of meaning in the humanities is loss of the future or, in other words, the prospect of progress and improvement of the human condition that has endured throughout history. The modern humanities conjugated their meaning in the future tense. How can they do this today, in the posthumous condition, when the linearity of time is taking us to a non-future?

In the eighteenth and nineteenth centuries, when the human sciences and sciences of the spirit took shape as the sphere of working out the meaning of human experience through the thought and educational proposals of authors like Kant, Dilthey, and Hegel, history was their stage and, accordingly, historical time was their medium. Kant was the great architect of this narrative when, in *What Is Enlightenment?*, he said that we are no longer in an enlightened age but in an age of enlightenment, by which he meant that emancipation through autonomy of knowledge (dare to know) is not a static condition but a dynamic one, a path of progress or, in other words, an always unfinished path of moral improvement. Later, Marx made of this dynamism a revolutionary demand and, of history, the antagonistic and contradictory transcript of the self-education of the human species. Then, however, liberalism translated this moral progress into terms of dynamism in economic growth and the social betterment of individuals. Progress thus became prosperity. Now, already unsustainable, prosperity is what threatens us.

Criticism of modernity and cultural servitude declared invalid the linear narrative of human improvement, together with the associated concepts of progress, historical meaning, and revolution. Postmodern criticism opened up the possibility of another experience of change which, since it is not subject to the linearity of a single view of history, is also open to other cultural experiences, other temporalities, and freer constructions of meaning. Learning no longer promised a better future, perhaps, but it did hold out a space for experimentation and creation of different and non-reducible possibilities of life.

With the change of century and millennium, with the economic, environmental, and civilisational crisis, the liberal version of the modern narrative, which is based on endless prosperity, is not only being called into question, but also the possibilities opened up by postmodern criticism have been taken over by destruction and fear. From the postmodern condition, we have gone to the posthumous condition, as I described earlier. This is the one that comes after the after, and it is characterised by the impossibility of any effective intervention in the conditions of *liveable* time (of human time, which is the time of history). What remains, then, is no longer time that adds but a time that subtracts, a time that does not open but that closes possibilities and ways of life.

Without a future, which is to say a horizon of progress and improvement, what can be contributed by the cultural legacy and tools of European humanism which, having started out from these premises, have seen them fail? The humanities, in the present debate over what the meaning of human is, cannot live on a repeated return to the future or, in other words, a defensive-nostalgic mindset based on prolonging and restoring a sense of history that is not only anachronistic but also, as I have shown, has a dark, Eurocentric side that preys on natural and cultural environments.

In this current dispute over what human might be, rather than going 'back to the future', as in the famous film trilogy, the first part of which was released in 1985, what we need is to work on the sense of temporality: instead of utopian promises and horizons, meaningful relations between the lived and the *liveable*, between what has happened, what has been lost, and what is yet to be done. More than giving us back the future, humanistic activities, in all their expressions, are the place from which we can appropriate *liveable* time, its shared, reciprocal, and egalitarian conditions, with regard to the singularity of each form of life and, inseparably too, on a planetary scale. Against apocalyptic dogma and messianic or solutionist monochrony (either damnation or salvation), the sense of learning is to work in an alliance of knowledges that combine scepticism and trust. I imagine the new radical enlightenment as the work of rebellious weavers, sceptical and trusting at the same time. We are capable of saying we do not believe you, while, from many places, we refashion the threads of time and of the world with fine-tuned, inexhaustible tools.

Part 2

PHILOSOPHY FOR A COMMON WORLD

1

How Not to Philosophise

People often ask me if I feel that I'm a philosopher and how I came to be one. To question someone who works as a philosopher is to question the person. I'm not sure that dentists would be asked if they feel that they are dentists, or engineers if they feel that they are engineers. But philosophy suggests an always open 'why?' about a vital decision. More than being linked with a profession or a field of study, philosophical activity is a possibility that one opts for as a way of life. It has personal but also collective consequences, for the environment and for one's own times. Is it possible to make this choice today?

Asking me if I feel like a philosopher and how I came to be one is also asking ourselves about the possibility and place of philosophy in our society. Our society is not something abstract. It is our schools and universities, and also our concerns, our conversations, and our ways of relating with what is happening. Philosophy is the *mania* of some, but it necessarily concerns everyone.

I started studying philosophy at a time when the institutional sidelining of philosophy went hand in hand with a widely accepted discourse about the end of philosophy. Moreover, this was happening in a country with languages – Catalan and Spanish, in my case – that do not have a strong philosophical tradition. Hence, what had never quite managed to begin was, oddly enough, arriving when it was ending. At the time, in the early 1990s, opting for philosophy was, therefore, going into limbo. It is now twenty-five years since that initial moment. The institutional sidelining of philosophy not only persists, but its effects are spreading in the school and university systems. The death of philosophy has not come to pass, however; rather, we are seeing the opposite. Philosophy was born in the open air, and it is returning to the streets. It was born in discussion and is being discussed again. It opened up as a chance for debate in a war between cities and ways of life. And now we are living with the evidence that a war without tanks has led our ways of life into serious conflict.

Opting for philosophy today means rebelling against its impossibility and death. All too often, this has been translated into justificatory positions in the defence of philosophy, which essentially mean playing the victim, as if it were an endangered species that should be preserved in a zoo. But philosophy does not need to be justified, let alone be preserved. On the contrary, it needs to be practised and propounded. It means leaving the place where its death was decreed to rediscover the need for it. As early as 1978, the Hungarian philosopher Agnes Heller wrote, 'The need for philosophy grows and grows: only philosophy itself does not yet know this.'*

However, philosophy is nothing if it is isolated. It is not locked up in its works, or encapsulated in academic courses, or limited by the set of professions that are supposedly concerned with philosophy. It is a practice of life that shifts the limits of what is visible and thinkable in every era, and for every historical and social context, starting out from a question about a truth that must be looked for in thought. It is not a gratuitous or frivolous activity. It is excess, yes, and, in this sense, a luxury, but its excess is about emptiness and desire: the impossibility of filling human existence with meaning and guidance. From this impossibility of unity and immediacy there emerges the desire for a truth that will be a guide for life, a knowledge that will, at the same time, be able to propose a way of life.

* Agnes Heller, *A Radical Philosophy*, Oxford: Basil Blackwell, 1984 [1978], p. 51.

There is a mismatch or a gap between life and its possibilities, between facts and values, between what there is and what there should be, between what we know and what we understand is escaping us, even if we do not know what it is. The mismatch list is infinite because these gaps are many faces of the same distance: the one that the thought of a finite being covers at infinite speed. The finite being is us. It is what we – not knowing where it begins and where it ends – provisionally locate in space and time as us, humans. What are the limits and conditions for the possibility of the thought that rebels against its own finitude, and against its own limits? This is what thought does. It goes beyond what it is that we immediately are, though not to find any old thing but something that would, in some way, be truth.

From here, from this body-to-body combat of thought and our own limits, the question cannot be how to go on philosophising but how could we not philosophise. This is how, in 1964, Jean-François Lyotard ended his four lectures to first-year students in the Sorbonne. With the title *Pour quoi philosopher?* they concluded, after a rousing, compelling explanation about the need and desire for philosophy, with the question, 'How not philosophize?'* As Lyotard shows, there are strong arguments in favour of the existence of philosophy, but they do not turn it into a more appealing or useful option for life than any other. It is simply unavoidable as long as we are willing to perceive the distance between us and the world and wish to name it. Hence, it is not a matter of tugging at the past of a moribund history but of being open to the present of an unfinished philosophy. This is a question, moreover, that presents, potentially to everyone, the challenge of philosophy. How not philosophise? This question is addressed to philosophers and non-philosophers, who come together in this shared power, which is the power of thought.

---

* Jean-François Lyotard, *Why Philosophize?*, trans. Andrew Brown, Cambridge: Polity, 2013.

Philosophy is like music. Some people practise it to the point of being virtuosos. Others are less formally involved. Some have in-depth knowledge of certain musical cultures and languages. Others are not so well informed. But all humans have some relation with music. It is the same with philosophy. You do not need to have read Plato to plumb the depths of a question like, What is justice? You do not have to venture into Wittgenstein's sentences to understand the scope and importance of our silences and of everything we are unable to say. Does this mean that neither Plato nor Wittgenstein is necessary because we are natural philosophers? That would be as absurd as claiming that music would exist in us without being part of any well-developed musical legacy. But what music and philosophy have in common is the relationship between a minority practice and an experience shared by all of us. Music and philosophy are not special kinds of knowledge that you might have or might not have. Apart from devoting ourselves to music or philosophy, there is an experience of music and of philosophical thinking that is part of us, whether we like it or not. You cannot escape from music, and you cannot escape from philosophy.

To take this analogy, how absurd it would be to talk about the death of music, but this is what happened with philosophy throughout the twentieth century and even today. Yes, it is true that, in the school system, music has undergone a similar institutional sidelining that is also increasingly extreme. Musical studies have been reduced to an extra, after-school activity that can only be enjoyed by those with the time and money to indulge. Yet would it ever occur to anyone to imagine a society and a life without music? As for philosophy, we have played too much with this idea of a post-philosophical society or one with no philosophy.

Some people might object and argue that there are other ways to think about the always unfinished sense of human existence, for example, art or religion in their diversity of expressions. Religion holds out a horizon of transcendence and art, a here and now of an expression that can be projected beyond itself. Art, religion, and philosophy do not act as substitutes for each other. They are shared, are continued, and, depending on the case, battle with each other as antagonistic ways of being in the world. But what does not exist is a religious or artistic fix with regard to the philosophical, although theology and a certain aesthetics of existence may have presumed to achieve this.

What is the specificity of philosophy vis-à-vis these other ways of thinking about the unfinished sense of human existence? Unlike art and religion, philosophy is the expression of a singular voice in search of a shared meaning. In the religious experience, a singular voice is subsumed in a higher meaning, the experience of the sacred or insistence on the divine, which would work as a reference to and guarantee of a shared meaning. In art, the singular expression, although universally communicable, does not depend on the search for a shared line of argument. Philosophy strains this polarity between the singularity of the philosophical voice and the potential universality of its discourse. Each philosopher is one him, or one her, with his or her own name and life choices, and finite in the singularity of being a life. Yet, at the same time, thought is being offered from here, and invoked as a place for meeting with anybody, and thus with everybody.

Philosophy is born with its own name and makes this name habitable. We do not know the first architects or the first poets, but we do know the first philosophers, in a list of names that are more important than the texts themselves, many of which are lost. Thales, Anaximander, Anaxagoras, Heraclitus, Parmenides, and other pre-Socratic philosophers chart out a map of proper names as options of thought. These names are also signs of an egalitarian passion, which is that anyone can make these singular thoughts their own. My thought is not mine alone, as anybody can think it because I have thought it, and thus I offer it. This is the paradox of philosophy, its demandingness, and its generosity. This paradoxical relationship between the singular and the common is not just the way philosophy is put into practice, but it is also the most important question running through all its themes and all its epochs. The diversity of forms (in ethics, in aesthetics, scientific and political, etc.) points to the possibility of keeping open one and the same question: how to live a real life, how to think, how to act, how to behave with regard to a truth that is thinkable by and for everyone? It is a question moved by the desire to bring together what is separate without unifying it. It is the movement of the desire that unfolds into the movement of intelligence, a desire (*philein*) that does not translate into intelligence but into intellection. What has to be understood? The relation of what seems to have no relation. *Logos*, Heraclitus called it, the relation that gathers and separates, that discriminates and links, that even makes it possible to contemplate the living unity of opposites. Like desire itself.

This is why philosophy is life-transforming thought. It is a system of notions and an attitude. Philosophy is lived thinking. It offers no formulae or prescriptions, but it places each specific life in a situation of having to locate itself in its own affairs as common problems. In times such as ours, dominated by procedures, apps, and methodologies, it is becoming difficult to explain this special way philosophy has of transforming life. Since the nineteenth century, the concept of utility has restricted the sense of practicality. But not everything that is the practice and apprenticeship of life needs to be understood as useful or rejected as useless. Philosophy, like other expressions of art and the humanities, has, too often, needed to take refuge in the supposedly sublime limbo of uselessness. However, what could be more necessary than keeping open the possibility of questioning ourselves about our ways of life and our truths? How to live, how to think, how to act? Philosophy is neither useful nor useless. It is necessary, necessary for the particular life of each one of us, and necessary for the collective life of societies.

The origin of philosophy is in the realisation of one's own debility and impotence, wrote the Stoic Epictetus in the first century CE. From this always specific, incarnate experience of finitude emerges the always unfinished power of thought. The possibility of philosophy in its Western development – but also in other forms of non-Western thinking – opens up into an awareness of the distance between a certain idea of totality and the limits of human existence in relation to it. Hence philosophy includes, as a condition, the possibility of non-response or an always unfinished elaboration. It turns the limits of thought into a lever for being able to think. Some people think that philosophy amuses itself by playing around with unanswerable questions. Rather than unanswerable questions, philosophical discourse is concerned with problems for which we always need to forge new concepts, not because they do not have solutions but because they change their existential situation and their historical, social, cultural, and political contexts.

Rediscovering the need for philosophy does not mean, then, recovering its lost dignity, as if it were a matter of polishing up an old piece of jewellery. Rediscovering the need for philosophy means putting it in a situation, exposing the philosophical legacy and its challenges to the existential and material situation of our times. Philosophy is a form of engagement with the world. Beyond particular commitments, it takes on the commitment to make and to have a world. This is why its ultimate task, as Marx said in the spirit of the most classical philosophy, is to transform the world and not by means of recipes and models but by contending with existing ways of life from an actual awareness of other ways of thinking and living. All philosophy, starting out from a position in which values are at stake, is a critique of some ways of life and a recommendation of others. All philosophy means, therefore, a battle between worlds that aspires to make of the world the home of humanity. How then can we not philosophise, how can we not keep philosophising today? This question is now taking on a tone of urgency.

Unfinished philosophy challenges us today in a world that is showing signs of exhaustion, as a planet and as a model of society. It is unfinished philosophy for an exhausted world. This is the challenge I propose to share here: from the threat of an end, learning to think and live finitude. Humans are finite, but not only us, for the totality itself is finite. This is a new meaning of totality, the total end of everything, for which we have no concepts, and which raises new problems. It is not a matter of intoning some kind of apocalyptic discourse, a practice as old as culture itself, but thinking in a way that is adequate for this real possibility. This changes the meaning of action, of values, of existence, and of humanity, as a species and as a subject.

Here I explore the place, or places, of unfinished philosophy in an exhausted world. Perhaps the main challenge of philosophy today is to *unfinish* the world. I do not mean saving it because 'saving' belongs to apocalyptic discourse, which moves between destruction and salvation in a binary scheme of extreme alternatives which, in the end, can only be decided by something that is beyond us, by God, history, or destiny. It's not about saving the world or humanity, but about making the world liveable and making humanity capable of accepting this challenge. As Epictetus said, being aware of our own weakness and impotence is our first step. Only from shared vulnerability will it be possible to launch a power of thought that is able to fight this tough battle.

2

From Infinite Universe to Exhausted Planet

The philosophical situation of our times is conditioned by a new experience of the limit, namely the limit that appears when human action can put an end to the very existence of humanity and of other species on this planet. Human finiteness, then, not only points to the mortal character of the human being but also acquires a new dimension: the finiteness of a species that can make itself extinct. Finiteness is not just a condition given by God or nature. It is the culmination of human action. The shattering of limits brings into being a new limit. This is Prometheus taken to the ultimate and most paradoxical consequences: wanting to do everything and being able to end everything.

In the 1950s, Günther Anders wrote about this paradox, the dual meaning of human annihilation by human productions. On the one hand, the invention of the atomic bomb in those years had become a reality that opened up the real possibility of the destruction of all human life at a single stroke. On the other hand, even if this does not happen, the very development of a world of technology also means the annihilation of humanity, which is trapped as quite a defective piece in its own system of instruments that discards humanity, surpasses it, and dominates it. So, 'the infinite is us' because our power of destruction is absolute. Yet twentieth-century humanity was starting to feel embarrassment and impotence at its smallness in the presence of the magnitude of its own work and the consequences thereof. Almost seventy years after these reflections on the obsolescence of man, the dimensions of the paradox have multiplied.[*] The shattering of limits no longer concerns only the disproportionate relationship between man and technology, but also the whole set of the human species' relations with the planet.

Henri Lefebvre wrote in 1965 that we have entered the planetary era, while also pondering the possibility of humanity's total self-destruction.[†] But even without the ultimate nuclear explosion, this self-destruction was already happening. It has other names and faces that disseminate the effects of the nuclear red button in space and time: contamination, climate change, depletion of natural and energy resources, destruction of the biosphere's diversity, and so on. The planetary era is the space-time in which everything is occurring as a situation shared by all humanity, over and above the diversity of its local political, social, and cultural contexts. Hence, taking and paraphrasing the title of Alexandre Koyré's important book, one might say that our era is that which has gone from the infinite universe to the exhausted planet.[‡]

In his book *From the Closed World to the Infinite Universe*, which was published in 1957, Koyré argues that the spiritual revolution of modernity was the destruction of the cosmos as an ordered, delimited, and hierarchical world and its replacement by an infinite and undefined universe. This universe, conquered by the new science, meant an expansion of the frontiers of thinkable and knowable reality but also a debasement of being, and a loss of humanity's place in the world. Without

---

[*] Günther Anders, *The Obsolescence of Man: On the Destruction of Life in the Epoch of the Third Industrial Revolution*, vol. 2, translated from the Spanish edition, available at libcom.org, 2014 [1980].

[†] Henri Lefebvre, *Metaphilosophy*, trans. David Fernbach, London: Verso, 2016.

[‡] Alexandre Koyré, *From the Closed World to the Infinite Universe*, Baltimore: Johns Hopkins University Press, 1957.

being anything more than matter and infinitely vast space, the universe no longer allowed the establishment of relationships of any value between the regions of the cosmos. Neither divinity nor goodness could be derived from physical facts. With the new physics, facts and values are divorced and so, too, are nature and history, and data and freedom. Hence, the relocation of humanity and its action in an infinite universe implies, at the same time, the birth of a human world as a dimension of a reality that does not belong to nature and cannot be measured by it. The human world is made by humans, and its only foundation is human freedom. It is a foundation that is not set in concrete but that opens up the being to what is to be done. Society and history, with all their political, cultural, scientific, and aesthetic manifestations, are what is being constructed. And the fact is that, starting from now, humanity has the task of making itself. Like the universe itself, this task is understood as an infinite one. Ever since Pico della Mirandola, with his Renaissance oration on the dignity of man, thinkers like Walter Benjamin who have been grappling with the painful breakdown of this same human world have been basing their work on this need to make of humanity itself an infinite task.[*] From the perfect finished infinite of God to the imperfect and always unfinished infinite of the human condition, this is the cut-off point for modernity in its quest for a new setting to develop a human life of dignity and sense, after the destruction of the Greco-Christian cosmos.

I believe that the only synthesis of these two experiences, that of the closed world and that of the infinite universe, is to be found in the ideological fiction engendered by the brief and fragile period of the so-called happy globalisation, which is how people were speaking of the world that was coming into being precisely at the end of the twentieth century. After the fall of the Berlin Wall in 1989, the transnational market

---

[*] Giovanni Pico della Mirandola, *Oration on the Dignity of Man*, trans. A. Robert Caponigri, Washington, DC: Regnery Gateway, 1996.

celebrated the end of the wounds that had made cracks in humanity's infinite task. At last, the world could be one again and, at the same time, infinite in the possibility of enjoying the eternal present of an economy with no other goal and no other dynamic than to keep going forever. The globalised world seemed to promise, once again, a cosmos for the individual consumer and customer, which was what all the planet's inhabitants would progressively become. But global mobilisation is a promise that requires going beyond what there is, in order to ratify reality itself.* This is how globalised capitalism and its prisons of the possible function: work, produce, consume in a world where there is no alternative. The infinite closes in on itself and the dark side of happy globalisation very quickly starts spreading its shadow.

Contamination, global warming, scarcity of natural resources, and new dangers: the twentieth century was not only the one of the Holocaust and Hiroshima. It was also that of Bhopal and Chernobyl. The twentieth century was one of world wars, mass extermination, and the Cold War. This is what the happy globalisation of markets seemed to have overcome forever. However, the twentieth century was also the one in which humanity's productive activity was so excessive that a few decades of it shrank all the previous history and the dimensions of the planet itself. In the last century, industrial production increased fifty-fold, the planet's population quadrupled and is still growing as well as being concentrated in ever-larger urban areas. In less than a hundred years, we have gone from an empty world to a full world, and not only because of increasing numbers of humans, but because this world is also full of predatory activity that turns everything it touches into a resource or waste. Resources are running out, and waste is accumulating non-stop. The data that give an overview of twentieth-century activity and its consequences

---

* Santiago López Petit, *La movilización global*, Madrid: Traficantes de sueños, 2009.

are blood-curdling. In a nutshell, the twentieth century used more energy than the whole history of humanity before then.[*]

As prestigious scientific institutions like the Geological Society of London and leading international publications recognise, we have entered a new historical-geological era characterised by humankind's impact on planet Earth. In 2000, Paul Crutzen, Nobel laureate in chemistry, named this era the 'Anthropocene', by which he meant the geological age in which the human species is the main driver of transformation of the physical constitution of the planet on the global scale. It seems that we have left behind the 12,000 years of relative ecosystemic stability known as the Holocene. If Günther Anders said then that the infinite is us, seventy years later we can say that, now, the planet is us. From the infinite universe to the exhausted planet, human history and natural history, which had parted in modernity, have come together again. The history of humanity no longer has a place in the world, but it, itself, *is* the history of the world.

This new intersection between the natural and the human, between history and nature, is now the field where the problems shared by the natural and social sciences are situated. This view is held by not only environmentalist thinkers like Serge Moscovici, who, since the 1970s, has stressed the historical character of nature, but also historians who are heirs of Marxism, like Dipesh Chakrabarty, and urban theorists like Mike Davis who, in essays like 'Welcome to the Next Epoch', speaks of the end of nature as an irreversible process of the intermingling of social and natural systems.[†] In a planet of megalopolises that shape a quasi-urban continuum, the city is no longer the opposite of rural but a socio-ecological

---

[*] J. R. McNeill, *Something New under the Sun: An Environmental History of the Twentieth-Century World*, New York: W. W. Norton, 2001.

[†] Mike Davis, 'Welcome to the Next Epoch', TomDispatch, 26 June 2008, tomdispatch.com.

system in which the future of the planet itself, or its total and self-conscious humanisation, is at stake. In his seminal essay, 'The Climate of History: Four Theses', which was published in 2009, Chakrabarty suggests something similar from the standpoint of history.* History is no longer the development of human freedom and creativity versus the atemporal, repetitive needs of nature. When, through its activity, the human species becomes the planet's main geological driver, human history is then the history of life on this planet.

This history is perceived today in the framework of a very real possibility of destruction of the planet and of life. Global warming of anthropogenic origin is the main sign of this, but other phenomena like contamination, extinction of the biosphere's diversity, and depletion of energy and natural resources must also be taken into account. In this dramatic encounter between human history and natural history, humanity finds itself in a new consciousness. In the infinite universe of modern science, humanity became both a stranger to matter and constructor of its own world. In the exhausted planet, humanity rediscovers itself as part of nature at a time when it is seen as its main destructive agent. Constructing its world, it destroys the planet. As I see it, this is the key to the philosophical situation of our times. In it, humanity is re-encountered as a specific negative universal. 'It is more like a universal that arises from a shared sense of a catastrophe ... We may provisionally call it a "negative universal history".' These are the words with which Chakrabarty concludes his essay. And, with these same words, we can return to the question of the current situation of philosophy and of its history, which is also threatened at this turn of the century by the shadow of an ending.

---

* Dipesh Chakrabarty, 'The Climate of History: Four Theses', *Critical Inquiry* 35, no. 2 (Winter 2009): pp. 197–222.

3

Philosophy Had a History

At least, that is what those of us who have been connected to philosophy in the last two centuries have believed. What did we study at school if not, most of all, the history of philosophy? How have textbooks, academic specialisations, and curricula been presented if not under the dictates of the stages of the history of philosophy and its leading figures? In the West, anyone with a modicum of education knows that philosophy originated in Greece and that it has at least three stages: ancient, medieval, and modern, although we are not very sure about what might have come later, if there is a later.

Oddly enough, in the East where, in theory, there has been no philosophy in the Greek sense of the word, and neither has there been any Western-style experience of history, it was understood that, in order to compete with the West in the philosophical domain, a history of philosophy was needed. Hence, between 1874 and 1923, first Japan and later China, produced what have been, to the present day, the works of reference in the history of Eastern philosophy, with their antiquity in the China of Confucius and Laozi among others, and their modernity in academically and technologically Europeanised Japan.

However, the notion that the matrix and meaning of all philosophy is contained in its history, its stages of development, and its evolutionary horizon is a recent invention, as recent as the same modern idea of History. From this framework, the idea of unfinishedness can only be understood as the crisis of a lineal development or as the stage that is yet to arrive.

Unfinished because of interruption or unfinished because it is incomplete, the unfinishedness of a story always goes back to the unity of its sense and development. But, if we situate the 'history of philosophy' framework within its own history and within its limits of validity, we will find that the meanings of the unfinishedness of philosophy are other and that they open up new territories to be explored, which are not necessarily marked by the threat of an ending or the linearity of a continuity.

One of the clichés that has come down to us through the conventional teaching of philosophy is that Aristotle wrote the first history of philosophy in Book I of *The Metaphysics*. In other words, philosophy would have begun as a history of itself. But is this necessarily the case? In the beginning of this work, one finds an account of the main ideas and contributions of the first Greek philosophers, including Plato. Here, Aristotle brings together the ideas of the philosophers who preceded him, the leading figures of the primordial, tentative science as he described it.

However, rather than a history of wisdom, I understand that what *The Metaphysics* presents is a narrative of collective learning. Knowledge of the first principles and causes, which is how Aristotle defines true wisdom, starts from a shared desire of the human being to know, and from an experience that some people make the starting point of their activity: admiration. Aristotle warns that although the desire to know is connatural to the human being, only those whose basic needs are already met, and who have the necessary freedom from worry, and the leisure to seek knowledge for its own sake, can freely indulge in it. Yet, for Aristotle, this freedom, which is a freedom in terms of ends (knowledge that has the end in itself, and not in any utility), does not mean that each person starts from scratch without any prior references. 'Every system of learning, however, subsists, or is attainable by means of previous knowledge, either of all things, or of certain particular things.'* What Aristotle is talking about in these pages is, therefore, an operation of gleaning, recognition, and evaluation of previous knowledge that must be taken into account. It is therefore a state of the question that would provide a solid base for his theory of the four causes. Previous knowledge does not consist, then, of theories with historical value or elements from an earlier stage, but it is comprised by approximations to a shared field of inquiry that, one way or another, express what we are looking for, separately and together.

What we can rescue from Book 1 of Aristotle's *The Metaphysics* is not the idea that philosophy has always been history of philosophy, but that there is no philosophising from square one, alone and out of time. Philosophy embraces the plurality of voices in time and listens to them out of a shared desire for truth. Its unfolding is temporal and collective, although its yearning for truth can be timeless and experienced individually. What accrues, from here, are positions, predecessors, compatible or rival schools, readings and interlocutors that are taken into account, discussed, and that are recommenced among themselves, again and again. It was not until the end of the eighteenth century, at least, that all of this came to constitute in Europe a history that was unified in meaning.

It was Hegel who gave philosophical form to the history of philosophy. He does not make of history an empirical concept, which would situate relationships in time, but presents it as being imbued with direction and meaning when he necessarily links the advance of reason and the development of universal history. This implies a clear locating of the starting point, the point of arrival, and the moments along the path of this history. This is what he emphatically does in his *Lectures on the History of Philosophy* (1833): 'Philosophy proper commences in the West.'† In these lectures, Hegel signals a historical cut-off

---

* Aristotle, *The Metaphysics*, trans. John H. McMahon, Mineola, NY: Dover, 2007, p. 33.

† G. W. F. Hegel, *Hegel's Lectures on the History of Philosophy*,

that amounts to a criterion of truth and identity. Philosophy is Western because, in his view, it was only in Greece that the encounter between the political freedom of a people and the freedom of thought of the individual took place. This, and no other, is the starting point of philosophy. And, from here, it is not only that the path of a historical journey is marked out, but also that the criterion for distinguishing between true and false philosophy appears. Only the form of thinking that, as principle and condition, embraces as its own freedom of thought with regard to all determination, end, or subjugation, is philosophy. From here, Hegel marked out the domains of philosophy in space and time. Any form of thinking that might have occurred before the Greek variant or outside the Western world might have had some connection with the development of the spirit and of universal humanity, but it is not true philosophy.

Hegel thus situates the history of philosophy between a before and an outside with which it has no relationship of either dialogue or continuity. Egypt and the Orient are not places for philosophy, neither territorially, nor politically, nor conceptually. Among people of the East, 'Conscience does not exist nor does morality. Everything is simply in a state of nature, which allows the noblest to exist as it does the worst. The conclusion to be derived from this is that no philosophic knowledge can be found here ... The Eastern form must therefore be excluded from the History of Philosophy ...'* The freedom that we see emerging only in Greece was to have its culmination in the modern Christian-Germanic world, the philosophical and political zenith of the universal history of humanity. If the history of philosophy has a beginning, it also has a goal. And Hegel believed he had found it in what his own philosophical-political context seemed to promise.

---

trans. Elizabeth Sanderson Haldane, vol. 1, London: Routledge & Kegan Paul, 1955 [1892], available at gutenberg.org.
   * Ibid.

It is clear that this kind of philosophical expression, rather than announcing the consummation of a history of freedom, had to be the harbinger of a time of disappointments, failures, and judgements. The culmination of philosophy as history soon became the historical crisis of philosophy. Hence, at the end of the nineteenth century, and for almost all of the twentieth, philosophers took up the question of the end of philosophy as a philosophical concern. Although we are now far from the dominance of Hegelianism and its schemes, it is evident that we have not overcome this impasse. What is there beyond the last stage of philosophy as history? Ever since then, philosophy has constantly been obliged to justify its continuity. In addition to having to define its task and its contours, its problems and its interlocutors, contemporary philosophy has become a repetitive intoning of self-condemnation and self-justification.

From the ordered, timeless space of metaphysics to the flow of time channelled by memory, philosophy has become a great archive of unfulfilled promises. Is remembering them updating them? It would seem – and some have asserted this – that this is the only task left to philosophy: unfinishedness as repetition and remembrance of an exhausted but unaccomplished history.

However, there is another option, namely, reviewing philosophy's relation to time and to its history, to open up new frameworks of understanding and evaluating philosophical questioning, and going beyond the scheme defined by a beginning and an ending, surrounded by a pre-philosophical before and a non-philosophical outside, and organised as a lineal route running through stages. This has been one of the main tasks of contemporary philosophy, from Nietzsche and Heidegger, each of whom, in his own way, again takes up the temporality of philosophy in a non-historicist sense. The time of truth is the time of an event that interrupts history. Our relationship with truth, Nietzsche would say, is of the order of creation, of the creation of new forms and possibilities of life. To this, Heidegger would reply that our relationship with truth

71

happens in the time of a revealing. We can only be ready for it, actively await it, make ourselves able to receive it and welcome it. For both Nietzsche and Heidegger, history no longer situates us. The event is an interruption of the flow of continuous time.

Yet this conception of truth as an event inevitably raises a problem. Why does it happen in some places and not in others? Why does it occur in some epochs and not in others? Why is it spoken in some languages and not in others? Why is not philosophy always and everywhere? More than a history tied to an identity, philosophy, in order to exist, depends on a *medium*, or an environment or, in other words, a set of conditions. This is what Gilles Deleuze and Felix Guattari talk about in the chapter 'Geophilosophy' in the book they co-authored in the 1990s, *What Is Philosophy?* They say that the medium makes philosophy. Geophilosophy 'wrests history from the cult of necessity in order to stress the irreducibility of contingency. It wrests it from the cult of origins in order to affirm the power of a "milieu" … It wrests it from structures in order to trace the lines of flight that pass through the Greek world across the Mediterranean'.* As Deleuze and Guattari see it, philosophy did not begin in Greece but, instead, something important related to philosophy occurred in the Greek milieu, so they recommend moving from historiography to geography, although perhaps it would be more accurate to speak directly of philosophical environmentalism. More than geography, which is mappable in space, philosophy has to do with environments and with the way they are arranged in space across time. No milieu is stable or permanently locatable. They are systems of balance, characterised by coincidence, fragility, and change.

By developing this environmentalist approach to philosophy, I believe we can resolve two problems. First, we go beyond the

---

* Gilles Deleuze and Félix Guattari, *What Is Philosophy?*, trans. Hugh Tomlinson and Graham Burchell, New York: Columbia University Press, 1994, p. 96.

exhausted framework of the history of philosophy without abolishing the relationship of philosophical thought with temporality and place. Philosophy is a kind of discourse that incorporates and makes its own the temporal dimension of experience. As Aristotle noted in *The Metaphysics*, there is always a before, predecessors and interlocutors in the joint search for truth. Even the *before* of a philosophy with its own name, which is to say the Egyptian and Oriental sources of Greek culture, become present and leave their traces in the very formation of philosophical culture. Moreover, the philosophical voice is temporal because it is not the voice of a revealed or eternal word of the sacred or divine type, but the plural voice of mortals confronted with their finiteness and the impossibility of saying, forevermore, everything. This is why philosophy needs permanent updating. It begins anew in each philosophical life, while at the same time taking up again past voices, their challenges, and what was left unthought. For Lyotard, 'The origin of philosophy is today.' Therefore, 'desire for unity attests to the absent unity', and 'what unfolds the fan of history is lack of unity'.*

The second problem that an environmentalist approach to philosophy can remove is that of thinking as an unpredictable event. Conceiving the possibility of thinking almost as a divine grace, Heidegger ends up referring to it as a gift or a calling we can only hope for as a new destiny for a West that is sunk in nihilism. Even Deleuze and Guattari use the word 'grace' at one point in their 'Geophilosophy' chapter. Then, what I now wonder is this: if the fact that there is philosophy is, in the end, a matter of grace ... if there is no philosophy, is this simply a dis-grace, in the sense of abasement or debacle? Thinking of philosophy in environmentalist terms enables more complex analysis of the material, cultural, political, and symbolic conditions that contribute to the presence of a more or less intense,

---

* Jean-François Lyotard, *Why Philosophize?*, Cambridge: Polity, 2013, pp. 65–8.

more or less creative, more or less interesting philosophical activity at any particular moment or in any particular place.

For those of us who come from historical-social contexts that are not much given to philosophical matters, for example the Iberian Peninsula and its languages, this is a challenging approach. Instead of wallowing in the victimism or defeatism of having been relegated in the great and necessary history of philosophy, or of not having been blessed by the grace of philosophical truth without knowing exactly why, we can wonder why and how philosophy has not appeared here in a recognisable form, and about the other forms of expression with which the essential questions about our unfinished existence have had to disguise themselves.

4

Doing Away with Philosophy

The passion for doing away with philosophy has accompanied philosophical activity, as an external threat and internal questioning. The external threat is part of the founding myth of Greek philosophy: the death sentence that the city laws decreed for Socrates. He was not killed by a madman or a rejected lover but by the legal system of the city. The defence of order was publicly expressed through the death of Socrates, who was accused of corrupting the ideas of the young.

This zeal of the guarantors of social order to eliminate philosophy has persisted through to the present day. The closest version of it is to be found in a series of educational reforms which, clearly in Spain but also in other countries, downgrade the study of philosophy to the status of an oddity in the humanities, while making space for what, today, bolsters order: expert knowledge, entrepreneurship, economic management, and even, once again, religion. But this threat, this see-sawing between philosophy's public acceptance and clandestinity, between promotion and condemnation, is part of philosophy's existence and, rather than being alarmed or scandalised, we need to know how to contextualise each historical moment and respond to it intelligently and appropriately. There is no golden past of philosophy, but only more favourable or more hostile milieus which, at any point, can go from one situation to its opposite. The philosophical situation, even at its most brilliant, is always fragile. If philosophy ceases to be public today, then we must develop a guerrilla version that will make philosophy spread and appear where it is not expected.

Yet, strangely enough, the passion to do away with philosophy has also come to be part of philosophy's own activity. In the nineteenth and twentieth centuries, in particular, philosophy itself became one of the main questions about the end of philosophy, and this was a task that had to be dealt with philosophically. As Pascal wrote in the seventeenth century, mocking philosophy is to be a true philosopher. In subsequent times, this idea was radicalised to such an extent that, in 1843, Feuerbach averred that the culmination of the art of philosophy happens when the philosopher gives up being a philosopher.

In what sense might modern philosophy feel the need to end itself? Any philosophical commitment contains a discrepancy, an imbalance between what there is and what can be thought, between thinking and doing, between the will of the whole, of the absolute, and the finite experience of the part or particularity, and so on. Theoretical monsters grow from this mismatch, feeding on practical frustrations. Philosophy does not seem to deliver what it promises, or it gets mired in its hypertrophied claims to possess the truth.

Modern philosophy is traversed by protest against this situation in two ways. Some people understand that ending this situation means putting an end to philosophy, bringing it to a conclusion, finishing the task that is still at its starting point, which is none other than reconciling thought with reality, and seeking some kind of settlement between being and thinking. Others think that ending what is not yet finished in philosophy, terminating this situation, would require doing away with errors, deviations, overreaching, and the violence that is intrinsic to philosophy itself.

The first is the way of Hegel and, in another sense, of Marx. Putting an end to philosophy means engaging in philosophy. Although they would not understand this engagement in the same way, for both of them and for all of those who, with them, have staunchly stayed with this possibility, there is a philosophical task that consists in finally doing philosophy. For Hegel, this is a conceptual task that evolves through the collective history of humankind. It is, therefore, a logical-political operation that entails both logical understanding of the order of the real, and its juridical ordering in the rational political form of the modern state. Understanding of the logical and ontological order, and the ethical-political ordering of collective life, being and what should be, logic, ontology, ethics, and politics thus come together in one and the same possibility for development, through to the end and without dark areas, of the rationality of the world as the achievement of freedom for humanity as a whole.

For Marx, this rational operation is necessarily revolutionary as the contradictions in which reality and thought are enmeshed are not conceptual or logical but social. The contradiction is class struggle, the error of understanding is ideology, and the accomplishment of philosophy, as reconciliatory understanding of being and thinking, of what there is and what we can think, is revolution: the revolution as truth to be produced. Hence, the famous sentence from *Theses on Feuerbach* about philosophers going beyond the task of interpreting the world to change it. What is not made clear in this thesis is whether or not the task of changing the world is also a philosophical undertaking. The sentence is open to both interpretations: going beyond philosophy as its cancellation or as its culmination in practice. Hence, two quite clearly opposing positions have arisen in Marxism, that of a positivist and activist anti-philosophy that denies that the conceptual task has any value, and that of a post-philosophy that again takes up the initial relationship of theory and praxis, as the living and never exhausted heart of philosophy. If we recall that Marx did his doctoral research precisely on Epicurus, one of the greatest exponents of the inseparable relationship between theory and praxis in the philosophical life, it seems clear that a simple condemnation and shutting down of philosophy cannot be ascribed to him but, rather, a demand for truthfulness. The revolutionary demand pitted against the temptation of theory. Philosophy only makes sense if it serves to change life or, as Epicurus would say, dispel fears, and be more amicable or, as Marx would say, overcome alienation and construct a classless society. This demand situates philosophy before the end of one history, and close to the start of another: the unfinished task of freeing life, through thought, from all the things that constrain it, including philosophy itself when it is unable to transform life.

Whatever their differences, both Hegel and Marx want to take philosophy through to the end, which means not keeping theory as separate but exploring the practical effects of a concept to the ultimate consequences. Battling against the separate, self-referential nature of the prevailing metaphysical tradition is also the main goal of other ways of approaching, in modernity, the need to put an end to philosophy or, rather, doing away with its errors, deviations, overreaching, and violence. If Hegel and Marx point out the non-fulfilment of the philosophical promise and set out to honour it, philosophers like Kant, Nietzsche, and, in the twentieth century, Husserl, Heidegger, Wittgenstein, and Deleuze, among many others, would point out the need for examining these promises, analysing their assumptions, critically scrutinising their possibilities and consequences and, on that basis, delimiting, rectifying, demystifying, and infiltrating philosophy itself.

Is philosophy dangerous, not only for the custodians of the social order but for itself as well? And what are the dangers that come with philosophical discourse? This is perhaps the question that runs through much of the relationship that modern and contemporary philosophy has had with itself. Since the Enlightenment, philosophy has discovered the need to engage in permanent self-criticism so as not to succumb to the errors philosophy itself creates. When neither the cosmic order nor the divine order assures the proper use of reason, how can the quest for truth be conducted properly? When everything ceases to be evident, how would it be possible to sustain a discourse that tries to think everything? The answer to this uneasy question will entail reconsidering precisely this endeavour and, in various ways, ending it.

This critical review of philosophy's claims to truth will be understood in three different ways. First, it would be a task of delimiting the spheres of philosophical certainty; second, a diagnosis of the truth value sought by philosophy; and third, a commitment to infinite rectification and repairing of philosophical activity itself. The first is the Kantian way, employed by much of modern philosophy until its radicalisation by Wittgenstein's call for silence about everything whereof we cannot speak. This consists of delimiting the sphere of meaning, assuming that philosophy cannot speak with any certainty about everything and that the desire for the absolute must, therefore, be relocated outside the discussion about what there is, in the sense of duty, for Kant, or in the experience of the ineffable, for Wittgenstein. The response, in any case, is the partitioning of discourse and diversification of realms of experience, as an analytical, critical method to avoid falling prey to the confusions of metaphysical philosophy.

The second way is the Nietzschean option, which is at the basis of all the standpoints that have approached philosophy from suspicions about its purported clarity and seeking in its dark areas the strengths, intentions, and power relations that motivate it. What is it that moves philosophy's always unsatisfied yearning for truth? Nietzsche asks the question as the physician of a culture doomed to the frustration of its own intentions, and thus to the sadness and resentment hiding beneath theoretical hubris. From this critical task of diagnosis and evaluation, Nietzsche proposes a leap, another philosophy, criticism as the threshold of creating new possibilities for life and thought. Only if we demystify philosophy itself will we be able to think radically again, cured of prejudices we have forgotten about. This relationship between demolition and creation is the second task taken on by philosophy as permanent self-criticism. In the second half of the twentieth century, a good part of French philosophy, notably including Gilles Deleuze, Michel Foucault, and Jacques Derrida, embraced this option.

Finally, the third way is that advocated by Husserl, Heidegger, and some of the leading German philosophers of the twentieth century. Their positions argue for the need to rectify the course taken by philosophy and to repair its consequences. Philosophy, as the aspiration of reason to think everything, can go astray. This is what Husserl famously stated in 1935: 'the European crisis has its roots in a mistaken rationalism.'* Mistaken in the blindness of scientific naturalism, philosophy can no longer think except in subordination to the object, to the datum, and to the technical product. This is philosophy alienated in the thing. But like any deviation, it can review the path it has taken, detect the error, and resume the march of thought in a different direction. This is still Husserl's trust in philosophy as a universal science, as knowledge of the whole, whose infinite, always unfinished task remains to be taken up again.

Heidegger extended the diagnosis of philosophy's straying into scientific blindness to the metaphysical conception that underlies it and is the reason why we only know how to think of being as a thing or as a set of things. The straying, therefore, began in Greece, and rectifying it means taking a gigantic leap backwards to start all over again and ask the question, this time properly, about being. Putting an end to the errors of philosophy means retracing its steps and thus being able to listen to, and once again engaging with, its first babblings. However, Heidegger himself eventually came to distrust this possibility and turned philosophy into a mere journey towards this

* Edmund Husserl, *Phenomenology and the Crisis of Philosophy*, New York: Harper & Row, 1965, p. 179.

improbable possibility, into a listening that is a waiting, and a commitment that is a willingness to accept that this – this starting again – might happen. It is the endless end of a philosophy that is exposed to the impossibility of truly thinking.

This mistrust, this uneasy despair is also to be heard in other philosophical voices of twentieth-century Germany, among them the thinkers of the Frankfurt School, including Benjamin, Adorno, and Horkheimer. Adorno was to synthesise this aporia of philosophy in the following idea: it is not that philosophy has taken the wrong path because of scientism, or that metaphysics is an error we can escape from if we go back to the beginning. The fact is that philosophy does harm and cannot not do harm. The concept, which is its tool, captures, totalises, and identifies what it names, and it cannot avoid doing so. The concept dominates the reality it touches on and falsifies it. Can we escape from being philosophically condemned to harming reality and harming ourselves in the process? Can we put a radical end to philosophy? Adorno would say we cannot, that this is just another trap, as inevitable as the first one. It would mean believing that there is an irrational, virginal, spontaneous outside, safe from conceptual thought and its pretensions of rationalising the world. Nothing and nobody, then, can save us from philosophy. Yet, as Adorno argues, we can heal the wounds it inflicts and, in doing so heal ourselves. This, and no other, is the never-ending, always unfinished task. It is the contemplative, self-critical task in which philosophical thinking has evolved, from the moment that it discovered that clear and distinct ideas also cast shadows.

Although the contrary would seem to be true, I believe that, when philosophy takes the position of putting an end to itself, it expresses confidence more than defeat, confidence in being able to honour its promises, or to take them further, somewhere else, using other ways of putting thought into practice. It is essential to understand today that the end of philosophy is not an announcement of closure or shutting down but, rather, the discovery of new territories for philosophical thought. As Deleuze said, it is necessary to leave philosophy with philosophy itself. This is the departure that contemporary thought is faced with, at the risk of losing itself. It is a departure leading to contagion with other languages, territories, cultures, and ways of thinking, a departure that is a shock, a straying that is no longer a mistake. After the end of philosophy, there is no longer any peace for philosophy. Far from having died, it has disseminated its seeds and grows, sometimes battered, sometimes dazzling, in places where it is not necessarily legitimised and recognised. This means exploring foreign territories, leaving Europe and Eurocentrism behind, opening our ears to languages that have not been dominant in the history of philosophy, and accepting as philosophical practices of expression, of writing, of encounter, and of creation that would not fit with what is being learned today in the classrooms of the philosophy faculties in the global university system. The dominions of philosophy must be made to overflow. These are times of philosophy *without dominion*.

5

'Europe Is Indefensible'

These are the words with which the Martinican poet and politician Aimé Césaire opened his famous *Discourse on Colonialism* in 1950. Europe's indefensibility was not just a matter of war, as in the Second World War, but also a question of civilisation: it was indefensible in showing that it was incapable of solving the problems it created and of justifying itself before the court of reason and conscience. These problems, with which Europe revealed its limits, were, for Aimé Césaire, proletarianisation and colonisation or, in other words, the two sides of the coin of modern capitalist imperialism: exploitation of workers and appropriation of populations, resources, and territories all around the world.

As the Peruvian thinker Aníbal Quijano has explained in recent decades, coloniality is not just one more fact of capitalist exploitation, but the pattern of global domination of the modern world-system that was hatched by capitalism at the beginning of the fifteenth century. It was not mere expansion. It was a new way of exercising domination over work, starting with a racial classification of the world. Race, says Quijano, is the first social category of modernity. Accordingly, Enrique Dussel argues, also from the Latin American point of view, modern philosophy did not begin with Descartes, all rugged up and huddled by his stove in Amsterdam, but with the conquest of the Americas, and the legal-philosophical debates that arose from the violence and the newness of the encounter. The need to justify civilisational superiority, and thus material, political, cultural, and religious domination of the colonised peoples broke with the old Aristotelian scheme of a world locked into its order and closed in on itself. The world was to open up, not only because of the discoveries in astronomy of Renaissance science, but also because of the reshaping of universality around the experience of the conquest of the Americas, and the history that all of Europe unleashed from then on until the present day. The idea of universality, core of European philosophy and religion, was embodied in a project of political and economic dominance of the whole world that has configured what the African American thinker Cornel West has called the 'age of Europe', which he situates between 1492 and 1945. Before 1492, Europe was not the only world centre but a crossroads between empires. From 1492 onwards, European modernity and its matrix of colonial power got underway, starting from the Iberian Peninsula.

The crisis of Western philosophy is inseparable from the end of the crisis of imperialism as the historical and spiritual form of coloniality. The crisis of Western philosophy is inseparable, then, from the end of the 'age of Europe' in a world where the West can no longer justify and solve the problems created by its domination of the planet and its version of universality. 'If there is any philosophy in the future, it will have to be born outside Europe, or as a consequence of encounters and clashes between Europe and non-Europe.'* These words come from a discussion Foucault had with a Japanese monk in 1978. If colonialism has been a history of these encounters and clashes in their most violent form, the twentieth century is one of mutation: from the colonial order to the global order. Europe is no longer the metropole, but there is no corner of the world that has not come into contact with Western culture and that has not been directly conditioned by it and its economic and political order. In the equally violent global order, there is no longer

* Michel Foucault, 'Entretien avec des bonzes', in *Dits et écrits*, vol. 2, 1954–1988, Paris: Gallimard, 2001, p. 618.

a single centre of political, economic, and political power, but neither is there an outside. This is why, Foucault says in the same conversation, 'the crisis of European thought has come to the attention of and concerns the whole world. It is a crisis that has an influence on the ways of thinking of all the countries of the world, and also the general thinking of the world.'*

In this sense, the global order is notable for a twofold displacement: first, what has been called Europe's provincialisation; and, second, the uncoupling of globalisation and Westernisation. They are two sides of the same process of decentralisation that calls into question Europe's singularity, its privilege as bearer of universal values, and the lineal story of its historic triumph over the rest of the world. In 2007, the Indian historian Dipesh Chakrabarty took up Hans-Georg Gadamer's notion of a provincialised Europe to argue for a general conception of the world, as a global world that is on the margins of Europe, or capable of situating Europe on the margins. 'To "provincialize" Europe was precisely to find out how and in what sense European ideas that were universal were also, at one and the same time, drawn from very particular intellectual and historical traditions that could not claim any universal validity. It was to ask a question about how thought was related to place. Can thought transcend its place of origin?'†

To provincialise is to decentre and contextualise. The European universal is the expression of one local culture among others. Acknowledging this does not mean succumbing to relativism or to the cult of particularism. As I see it, the important thing is to investigate the conditions that have made possible the Western mirage and its material effects on the fate of the whole planet. Philosophy is at the heart of this mirage, so it is impossible to decolonise the world without decolonising

---

* Ibid.

† Dipesh Chakrabarty, preface to the 2007 edition, *Provincializing Europe: Postcolonial Thought and Historical Difference*, Princeton, NJ: Princeton University Press, 2007 [2000], p. xiii.

philosophy. The key question is the one that Chakrabarty identifies: place of origin. And what if singularity of the place of origin is the myth with which Europe has colonised the world? Europe makes of its particularity a singularity that will save the world. Only in Europe was rational thought and democracy born, only in Europe did Christianity and its message of love for humanity consolidate, and only in Europe did the birth of capitalism and the industrial revolution occur. Paradoxically, this uniqueness makes Europe the shared destiny of humanity, and the 'diffusionism' of its ways of life humanity's only motor of progress.* The historical consequences of this destiny and its imposition cannot be fought without dismantling this myth of European singularity. This would entail the encounter between the critical internal and external, European and non-European points of view, of which Foucault spoke with the Buddhist monk.

But, let us be careful, 'the European' is a historical construct that is also violent towards the very inhabitants, people, languages, and the social and human realities that have made up the multiplicity of forms of life in the territories of the continent of Europe. The 'European' has been imposed on Europeans, and we should not forget this. Dismantling the uniqueness of Europe and its triple Greek-Christian-capitalist origins is essential for the emancipation not only of colonised peoples but also of Europe's specific realities. Who, in Europe, are the excluded, exploited, and ill-treated of its triumphal history? What came before and what was left out of the supposed Greek miracle? Why have Egypt and Mesopotamia always been the rejected shadows, the unacknowledged background of the beginnings of some civilisations – European civilisations – that would later break away so as to no longer recognise that they were related? And what are (permanently) the heresies and infidels of a West that needs to delimit in blood and fire the

* This term is analysed by J. M. Blaut in *Geographical Diffusionism and Eurocentric History*, New York: Guilford Press, 1993.

contours of its allegedly universal identity? Asking these questions is not a matter of saving ourselves today through others but an attempt to find other ways of understanding ourselves vis-à-vis others.

In order to do this, we need to learn to listen to what modernity did not listen to, from inside and from outside of Europe at the same time. We must listen to what Europe did not include in its dominant narrative, but must also pay attention to the not-exclusively-European character of scientific, philosophical, technical, economic, and political modernity. From the perspective of the colonised, the modern world has always been a shared world. Although they were given one, hegemonic, Western voice, progress, technological and industrial development, and the modern visions of the world have been produced on the basis of forced but irreversible relations among territories, societies, and cultures. The colonised, as well as the colonisers, have constructed the modern world. With their work, their land, their knowledge, their despoliation, and also their rebellion. If there is something left unfinished in modernity, it is not its culmination as a project, as Habermas argued. It is listening to, being receptive to, and developing its silenced voices, its invisibilised viewpoints, and its neutralised presences.

For this, we also need to listen to and work side by side with thinkers who are presently working in all fields of non-Western modernity. Among many others, Wang Hui, author of the monumental *The Rise of Modern Chinese Thought*, argues for the idea of recurrent early modernities as a key notion from which to trace the vestiges of modernity which, in different parts of the world and outside of any lineal scheme, make it possible to understand the thinking of the present-day world and how it has developed. From here, the world is no longer understood on the basis of a universal history of humanity along historicist and Hegelian lines but, instead: 'The movement of the world is a process in which multiple spheres communicate and interpenetrate and mould one another.'* How, then, can we understand the European dominance of the last few centuries? Another thinker, in this case the British social anthropologist Jack Goody, suggests a model according to which, from the Bronze Age onwards, there would have been cyclical change in the relations of dominance among the world's different societies, especially in Eurasia.† On the basis of his highly specific studies on notions like individualism in family structures, food, and forms of exchange, Goody demonstrates that there is not one single, privileged route to modernity, and neither is modernisation a Western phenomenon transported to the rest of the world.

Radicalising even more this decolonisation of the Eurocentric idea of modernity, the African philosopher Achille Mbembe argues for the unfinished, incomplete nature of modernity, starting from the fact that colonisation has been 'the spectacle par excellence of the impossible community'. In its failure to offer a world order of coexistence, displaced Europe now places us in the position of being 'inheritors of the whole world' but 'at the same time, the world – this inheritance – has to be created'.‡ Hence the need to develop a 'world-thinking', a new universalisation of representations, an alternative to that of Western colonial modernity. This thought can no longer rest universalisation on the idea of unity or totality, but rather on interlinking that includes dislocation and proximity as allies. For this world-thinking, therefore, there are no centres or peripheries because every specific universality, beyond the general–particular duality, has incorporated its decentred condition.

The question that arises, and which we must take as crucial today, is whether philosophy can decentre itself without

---

* Wang Hui, 'Reclaiming Asia from the West: Rethinking Global History', *Asia-Pacific Journal* 3, no. 2 (2005), p. 5.

† Jack Goody, *The Eurasian Miracle*, Cambridge: Polity, 2009.

‡ Achille Mbembe, *Out of the Dark Night: Essays on Decolonization*, New York: Columbia University Press, 2021, pp. 2 and 63.

disintegrating. Philosophy was the core of this imperialist world centred above all on what was European and its rational domination of the world. Oddly, it was an empty centre, always on the move, able to accommodate its absence of foundations under its aspiration of systematising totality. Yet, even so, this void worked as a centre and a centraliser. What happens when philosophical thought starts multiplying its places and there is no longer any centre of reference for discourse? The multiplying could be simple fragmentation, dispersion, or epistemological and cultural relativism. Or we can make of it the condition and starting point of the future philosophy that Foucault glimpsed as an as yet unfulfilled possibility.

6

The Places of Philosophy

Like economics, philosophy has gone global. What is not so clear is that this means neither the historical reconciliation of thought and the world, as Hegel glimpsed, nor the development of a world-thinking, as proposed, among others, by Achille Mbembe. What we do find with the current globalisation of philosophy are basically two phenomena. The first is the rather uniform nature of philosophy teaching in almost all the world's universities. The second is the effort to diversify the national or ethnic character of philosophical expressions in the local scene.

The first trend is related to the world as a global knowledge market. The neoliberal university conforms to a model that tends towards linguistic, epistemological, and ideological uniformity. The aim is to compete on the same ranking scale and encourage the circulation of a uniform profile of academics. In this situation, philosophy comes to function as just another discipline, and it has to play by the same rules of the game. The upshot is standardisation of thinking practices and the shrinking of philosophy to a schematic set of specialist currents which may be along historical, linguistic-analytical, or thematic (aesthetics, ethics, political philosophy, etc.) lines. In this framework, Western philosophy and its history are predominant, although there is an increasingly greater presence of recent sectorial incorporations like gender philosophy and place-based philosophies (Spanish, Chinese, and others). Apart from a few local variations, all philosophy faculties look increasingly alike.

The second trend is related to all the world's nations, peoples, and cultural identities. The modern world is organised as one consisting of nation-states, first of nation-states and their colonies, and then as a set of nation-states and their neocolonial relations of dependence and subordination. Likewise, in cultural terms, the modern world understands itself as a sum of peoples, side by side, each people with its own language and cultural identity. With this dual political and cultural map of the nation-state, philosophy is also nationalised and directly linked to the cultural identity of each people or state. Accordingly, Greek philosophy is no longer referred to as the philosophy that arose in Greece. Instead, people speak of Greek, French, English, or German philosophy as if it is philosophy that belongs to each corresponding people and within the framework of their states. Outside Europe, a twofold process is occurring: together with the exportation and imposition of the academic and ideological schemes and frameworks of Western philosophy, the existence of local philosophies – Chinese philosophy, Mayan philosophy, Bantu philosophy – is being recognised as a particularity. Depending on the case, the cultural or national adjective works to standardise philosophical expressions and views of the world by locking them into their identity enclave. Whether they are ancient or modern worldviews, located in small or large population groups, linked to religious, political, or scientific institutions, the important thing is to situate for each cultural-political identity a minimum conceptual nucleus that can be recognised as its philosophy.

This process of standardising peripheral or non-European philosophies can occur from two different standpoints, either as recognition, by analogy, of something similar to Western philosophy, or as an upholding of the philosophical abilities of every human community, albeit from parameters that have little in common with the pattern established by the history of Western philosophy. In the former case, one finds a distinction between philosophy in the strict sense (of Greek roots) and philosophy in the broad (of others) sense, or that between the pre-philosophical and the truly philosophical. From this stance of recognition, Western European philosophy continues to be the true philosophy, though it admits variants, resonances, and insights from other ways of thinking. However, the dual scheme separating self and other is at work, and imposes its dominance, whether in dialogue or in academic, publishing, and cultural relations.

Assertion of the fact that, on the basis of certain conditions of language and social organisation, all human communities have something we could equally fittingly call philosophy goes further. It breaks with the pattern where philosophy is seen as a Greek invention, which means it cannot function as an analogy. As Enrique Dussel writes in the introduction to the jointly authored volume *El pensamiento latino-americano, del Caribe y 'latino' (1300–2000)*, 'All peoples have problematic nuclei that are universal, consisting of the set of basic questions which *Homo sapiens* should have asked … when the human being was faced with the totality of the real, in order to be able to manage it and reproduce and develop human community life.'* From this viewpoint, the problematic nuclei cannot be absent in any culture or tradition, and they unfold in a range of conceptual narratives, but all of them are rational in the sense that they seek to find reasons for what they are talking about. Accordingly, philosophy was not born in Greece, and neither can Greek-born philosophy be taken as the prototype of philosophical discourse. It is a particular case that does not include a universal definition. The rebellion against the hegemony of 'dead white men' has the power to redefine the very notion of philosophy, but it has the result of creating a kind of philosophical multiculturalism that does not question the notion of cultural identity that underpins it.

---

* Enrique Dussel, Eduardo Mendieta, and Carmen Bohórquez, eds, *El pensamiento filosófico latinoamericano, del Caribe y 'latino' (1300–2000)*, Mexico City: Siglo XXI, 2009, p. 15.

Whether from the hierarchical stance of recognition or the rebellious one of a claim, we cannot ignore the fact that the map of globalised philosophy is still one of a world consisting of nations and their corresponding cultural identities. Philosophy, then, comes to be part of the cultural package of each people, which means reproduction of the map drawn since Romanticism by literary studies with its combination of national literatures in the framework of universal literature outlined by Goethe. Each nation has its language and literature, and they all flow together in the great temple of *Weltliteratur*, or universal literature. The production of canons, translation, and comparativism are all practices that make possible a relationship with literature as an expression of the spirit of humanity through the spirit of its peoples.

In this situation, I would ask if this map makes sense for philosophy. In his *Provincializing Europe: Postcolonial Thought and Historical Difference*, Dipesh Chakrabarty says that globalisation, as a process of Europe's provincialisation, means asking about the way in which thought relates to space, the conditions under which the forms of thought are connected with places, both in and beyond them. A true decolonisation of philosophy in a common world would therefore also require a redefinition of the world political space that goes beyond its organisation as a global market and set of national territories.

At this point, it is worth turning to Homi Bhabha and his critical analysis of the cultural-literary space, as it has been shaped in modernity and also in its subsequent phase. In *The Location of Culture* (1994), Bhabha suggests going to find culture at the fringes of nations and institutions, beneath the uniformity of the universal, and the homogeneity of national identity. This brings us to the edges, the limits, and transition zones, real and symbolic frontiers, refugee camps, linguistic hybridisation, the displaced, the migrants, and to homeless lives. Culture understood from the experience of inclemency does justice to the human truth of what Bhabha describes as an 'unhomely world'. Only from such a borderland vantage point does otherness stop being the phantom invoked by critical intellectuals comfortably installed in their centres of operation. In this interstitial space, where nothing welcomes us, the other finds a space of power, of being able to act, and appears as an 'agent of articulation'. The cultural diversity of the world of nations is swamped, then, by a cultural difference which is that of the unpresentable, that of oblique, off-centre, and disjunctive relationships. From there, it is possible to review not only the cultural fact but the human community itself. In the interstices, at the limits, at frontiers, what Bhabha calls the 'new internationalism' becomes possible. This is not based on transcendent schemes but goes from the particular to the general, 'a process of displacement and disjunction that does not totalize experience'.*

Going back to Bhabha's analysis, I believe that true philosophy is precisely the experience of this displacement from centres that mentally and materially organise personal and collective life and its identities. It can be captured as a global academic product, or as an expression of the cultural identity of each people, but philosophy won't be found there. A nicely presented embalmed body of discourse is there, but not the effect of thought. The geography of philosophy, then, is not that of the world of nations and institutions, but of frontiers and displaced people. A philosophical life is always out of place. Even if it hides under the cloak of the biography of a reputable professor, those of us who have, one way or another, been involved with philosophy know that something else is always going on with it. This other thing is what is communicable beyond linguistic and cultural differences, beyond religious, literary, and scientific traditions. It is about something that is very basic: the desire to understand everything and to do it for oneself and with others. This wish to 'give reason', which

---

* Homi K. Bhabha, *The Location of Culture*, London: Routledge, 1994, p. 5.

Dussel spoke of as a problematic nucleus that every human group inevitably develops, is not limited to being translated into a classifiable ethnic or cultural feature, along with others. Rather, it opens up a statement that can be addressed to any human being. In philosophy there is no inter-culturality but there is interpellation. This is the sense of the non-transcendent universality that Bhabha sought in interstices. It is also the universality of a not-knowing and of a silence that necessarily comes with the wish to understand everything.

In order to deploy its concept-creating activity, philosophy needs to move along the frontier between different kinds of scientific knowledge, along the limits between theory and practice, in the friction between the personal and the collective, through the zones of transit between cultural identities, and in the distance that ethically and politically separates what there is and what there should be. Therefore, philosophy itself is also the frontier that joins the philosophical and the non-philosophical, what is proper to it and not proper to it, because this is an interstitial zone that, with no place of its own, crosses through and opens up everything. It is the gap, the uninhabited space, that brings everything into relation. More than a single, universal truth, it must come to be the practice of this new internationalism of the displaced, and be able to trace the disjunctions without totalising the experience.

In his essay *Schopenhauer as Educator*, Nietzsche wrote, 'East and West are signs that somebody chalks up in front of us to fool such cowards as we are.'* The Eastern frontier is precisely the one that has both contained and externalised Europe's fears, from the Persian enemy of ancient Greece, through the Arab threat, to the 'yellow peril' of today's world. Dualisation of the world makes it possible to have an inside and an outside, oneself and an other. But, if we do this exercise of tracing on a map of the world the chalk line separating East

---

* Friedrich Nietzsche, *Schopenhauer as Educator*, trans. Adrian Collins [1874], available at wikisource.org.

from West, the chalk ends up smudging almost the entire Eurasian continent and, above all, leaves large parts of the world without a place, without a home within this partition. This frontier-world is what we have inherited in its entirety. All of it, whether we know it or not, is a transit zone, for both lives and goods. Taking a philosophical stance in this world requires that we stop ignoring this and instead make of its inhospitality our common situation, our shared world. This is the true common basis of experience.

Precisely with regard to the reception of Eastern philosophy by the West, there was an interesting discussion a few years ago by two leading French sinologists, François Jullien and Jean François Billeter. The former is known for his reading of Chinese philosophy as radical otherness, or the absolute outside of the Greco-Western framework of intelligibility. Taking up some Foucauldian notions, he refers to Chinese thought as a 'heterotopia', as a place without a place, the circling of which means a true distancing from everything that is thinkable for us. Jullien does not try to prevail over the truth of the other but to expose himself to the effects of the encounter with the other within his own framework of thought. These are the effects of a conceptual, linguistic, and temporal alienation that does not try to achieve mutual understanding but instead resonance with what is radically strange. In a small book published in 2006, Billeter objected to this interpretation. From a place which, at first sight, may seem to be that of a uniformising universalism, Billeter formulated a double question which, when listened to without prejudice, is unsettling. Are the Chinese really so different from us? Is there a common pool of experience?

I cannot answer these questions from direct knowledge of the other, since I have never set foot in China and neither can I read its literary and philosophical legacy in any way other than in translation. Yet many of the products I use in my everyday life must come from its factories and from its hands, as does the capital that finances Western governments and investments in the global market. So, are the Chinese really so different from us? Is there a common pool of experience? If there is, and we are not so different, it surely is not because of features that makes us equal from a certain conception of humanity or species, but because of the fact of our sharing the inhospitable nature of existence, and the unfinished status of our knowledge, and the fragility of our personal and collective projects. From the unfinishedness of this common world, we constitute cultures that are no longer mutually opaque or incomprehensible but different perspectives on a same, irreducible mural.

> I promised to show you a map you say but this is a mural
> then yes let it be these are small distinctions
> where do we see it from is the question[*]

This mural of infinite and irreducible distinctions is the topography where philosophical thought must rediscover its place of places. Only from here can philosophy cease to be an academic or cultural product and offer itself as an existential and political position.

Nevertheless, to find itself there again, in this unseemly position conquered on the boundaries of knowledge, institutions, and identities, philosophy will have to cross, and keep on crossing, many barriers. The main barrier today is its academic and epistemological entrapment. The university must be a platform, springboard, and connector of forms of knowledge and worlds. But the present drift of universities in the global knowledge market is going in exactly the opposite direction. One key question when it comes to considering the current development of a philosophy that is committed to the world must then be this: What is happening in the university today? What and who can think from the university system as it now functions?

---

[*] Adrienne Rich, 'An Atlas of the Difficult World', in *An Atlas of the Difficult World: Poems 1988–1991*, New York: W. W. Norton, 1991, p. 6.

7

Standardising Thought

In today's society, both inside and outside Europe, the presence of philosophy is concentrated mostly in secondary and tertiary education. It is generally assumed – and these are prejudices to be questioned – that children do not need to have any relationship with philosophy and that, outside a university education, there should only be, at most, media opinions and self-help books. Many scholars have analysed the visual dominance of our media culture, but we are still living in cultural milieus where discourse, even if it is no longer found in books, is omnipresent. People talk, argue, write, and read continually. Yet, this does not mean that we are in an open situation where a real debate of ideas is happening. Thinking is presented in a highly standardised way, in the form of opinions and political marketing slogans. The main enemy of philosophy has always been standardised opinion, what is thought and accepted without wondering why, in keeping with parameters of what is deemed socially thinkable and common sense. In Greece, opinion was called *doxa*. The problem is that this process of standardising thought also affects teaching and, more specifically still, academic activity in general. In the university, too, thought has become standardised.

Hence, the question about philosophy's place in the school and university has been raised again today as a matter of concern and urgency. It is evident that the transformation of educational institutions, the cutting of public budgets, and evolution of both knowledge and cultural markets are elements of a trend that is forcefully pushing in a single direction: the marginalisation of philosophy in educational curricula, in academic structures, and in university excellence rankings. However, though the question about philosophy's place may be urgent and pertinent today, it is not new. On the one hand, the present situation is no more than the culmination of a decades-long series of episodes of besiegement of areas of knowledge that are less profitable for universities. On the other hand, though, philosophy's relationship with academia has never been clear, and it has never enjoyed a single desirable or stable formula. Plato invented the Academy, but it has never been clear whether philosophy is academic, or whether it might be so in a sure and stable way for everyone, and in any political or social setting. So, philosophy is, once again, in an uncertain place. The history of this uncertainty is, in fact, its own history.

Unlike other highly specialised areas of knowledge, it has always been possible to relate to philosophy from different places, purposes, and levels of intensity. Philosophy can be studied in its history, read in its texts, frequented in its existential or cosmological questions, debated in its ethical and political consequences, consumed as part of general culture, used as a resource for developing models of thought applicable to other fields ... Philosophy can be known, mastered, enjoyed, instrumentalised, transmitted, sold, synthesised, popularised, and so on. This is why there are so many reasons for coming to a philosophy faculty and why so many different students turn up in them. And it is also why the habitat of philosophy has never been exclusively of the university or other such educational institutions.

Nevertheless, although the university is not the exclusive domain of philosophy, it is still the main channel for its propagation. And, in today's universities, thought is being asphyxiated. This looming threat of asphyxiation is not exclusive to philosophy. The possibility of making free, experimental thinking the basis of knowledge and scientific research in general is also in danger. It seems that the current drift of the global university not only accepts this asphyxia but is also willing to see it through to its ultimate consequences. Philosophy can bloom again in an open field, can acquire the instruments to reinvent itself, and in other places, as it has done on other occasions. But can the university, as the centre of higher education and research, take on the consequences of this asphyxia?

It is not only a matter denouncing the neoliberal, profit-driven trend of universities but also looking at how that trend affects specific ways of doing philosophy and relating to particular practices through which thought is elaborated. Philosophy is basically done by writing. It was born with writing and, although it embraces many other dimensions of life and relationships with the word, its medium and even its raw material is writing. Attention should therefore be given to the ways in which writing can be done in universities because it is in them that we find the keys to the standardisation of thought in present-day academia.

The real problem that appears in academia today is that of an apparent neutralisation of this conflict around the paper or scientific research article. Today, in the global university, every lecturer and researcher, from whatever the field, must be uniquely and exclusively a producer of scientific research articles that make their mark in terms of international research rankings. Books, essays, creation, cultural and social activity, and even university teaching itself have ceased to have any value. In other words, the university and also the activity of those who work in it are gradually disappearing. The paper – an item whose English name has now crept into all languages – this certain kind of article, is a highly precise standard of writing and relationship to writing. As a standard, it is not one way of writing among others, but one that presents parameters of validity and a recognised place of enunciation for any content that is seeking to be academically relevant. The effects on writing and, accordingly, on philosophical thought, are decisive.

First, in the paper, form and content are dissociated. Although we have picked up the bad habit of studying authors by separating 'doctrinal' content from the substance of their texts, in philosophical writing, form and content require each other and are inseparable. Dissociating them is precisely what turns philosophy into theoretical discourse and annuls its embodied and experimental nature. This means that the paper tends to silence the voice. This formal standard results in a hushing of the philosopher's own voice, and the erasure of his or her personhood in an already formatted text. Who speaks in a paper? To whom? It speaks to peers, other supposed experts in the field. The expert is the figure that fits the standardised language of academia and is therefore the only recognisable and appraisable type of academic in today's universities.

The second consequence of this standardisation of the place of enunciation and interlocutors of writing is annulment of experience. Experts do not make of writing a place of experience precisely because the only people who can venture into the experience of their own transformation are those who are willing to forsake what they already know. The expert has abandoned experience and its uncertainties for research and its results. This is what they write about. In philosophy, this means forgetting about any real kind of philosophical problem in favour of two kinds of *topics* (another widely adopted term from English):* either lines of research favoured by project evaluation bodies, in accordance with predetermined criteria of academic relevance usually dictated from other fields of knowledge, or turning authors of reference into objects of research rather than treating them as conversationalists in thought. The traditional academy was the place of scholars who devoted their lives to in-depth knowledge of an author, producing

---

* Translator's note: There is for a Spanish or Catalan reader, at least, the sense of 'cliché' in both *tópico* and *tòpic*.

monographic studies that aided and guided the work of others. Nowadays, this figure has become generalised, banalised, and imposed as the only possible one to emulate. The expert on an author, period, or school of thought is now not only the most common figure in European philosophy faculties but also the only recognised one. The academic in question is thus not the only one being silenced, because the original author, now become an object in the expert's career of specialist inquiry, is as well. In this double silencing, the experience of thought is neutralised.

Every standard leaves an outside, all that is excluded and not recognised by its parameters of legitimacy. Hence, the third consequence of the predominance of the scientific article as the centre of academic production is the delimiting of an inside and outside of writing. It is a dramatic, arbitrary, and violent split. The paper works as a unit of production, judgement, and evaluation of what is understood as research activity. But is also works as a boundary. As a standard, it excludes from the sphere of the acceptable, visible, judgeable, and evaluable any writing that does not comply with its objectives and protocols. A continuation of the split between communication for a community of experts and popularisation in the rest of society, all writing in the academic world has been harmed by this division. Scientists have the slogan 'publish or perish'. In the domain of 'letters', we could change the terms and ask the question: do you write, or do you publish? It would be a joke that portrays the dramatic situation of so many 'academics', and not just philosophers, who must choose between writing to publish within the framework that has been established for writing, or writing what they really need to think. In the case of philosophy, this demarcation has a twofold effect with consequences we have not yet evaluated sufficiently. On the one hand, the philosophy that enters the legitimised field of standardised writing is a philosophy that is placed in the absurd situation of having to present itself as scientific research. On the other hand, the remainder of philosophical writings ends up ascribed to either literature (the philosopher as writer) or journalism. The natural overlap between philosophy and literature, between the philosophical word and the poetic word, has, from the stronghold of today's university, been unambiguously forced out into extramural exile. And the relationship with the public word has been left to market forces in the arenas of communication and entertainment.

Finally, there is one more important consequence which, though it may seem to be anecdotal, is certainly not: rankings, established by Anglo-Saxon assessment and evaluation companies, reward publication in journals in their own linguistic and cultural sphere, which means that academic writing today is increasingly limited to English as its only language. Hence, the inside and outside of academic writing has a determinant linguistic aspect. The requirement that university activity must meet international standards of scientific production evidently entails its being increasingly communicated in English, not only in keeping with criteria of usefulness but also, directly, as part of its added value. When a language is simply a way of conveying findings, the language in which they are communicated may have relative importance. But does the same thing apply to philosophical writing and its creative, personal, and experimental singularity? Of course not. Given the mobile and delocalised character of its readers and discussants, philosophy in its Western, and specifically European, tradition has had a continuously shifting relationship with languages. Depending on epochs and the more intense foci of philosophical creation, one or other European language has predominated, but always in communication with others. There have been classical languages, *linguae francae*, languages with more philosophical prestige than others, and even hegemonic and proscribed languages, but there is never a neutral language. If doing philosophy means creating concepts and this, as I said, 'happens' by writing, then part of philosophy's raw material is the language in which it is written. Writing philosophy always entails a linguistic decision, a commitment to render the language, whether one's own or adopted, in a different way. Today, this decision is hobbled, blackmailed, and subordinated to calculation of a profit that is directly taken into account in an academic career, as well as in employment possibilities and institutional visibility.

In philosophy, then, the consequences of standardising academic writing around the paper are not just formal (how to write a scientific article) or related to institutional monopoly (where one is published and with what prestige), but they also patently affect the practice of philosophy and the conditions of its teaching. Given the situation I have just analysed, the question raised for university philosophy teachers is evident. Is teaching philosophy in a university about producing supposed experts and training students to write papers in which they can demonstrate their research expertise? Or is it something else? The first option means renouncing philosophy by pretending to do philosophy. The second means taking on a tough task, against the tide and in 'stealth'.

8

To Write Is to Be Transformed

In philosophy, writing is not a means of communicating ideas and knowledge but, rather, the raw material with which concepts and problems are elaborated. Philosophy is thinking that takes shape in writing, and the philosopher's voice is one that is remade in writing. This does not mean that philosophy is just a literary genre or that it ends with its own works, for writing is true if it connects with a way of life, rooted in a singular experience, and with a search for a common purpose. This connection opens up problems that are always new without needing to be innovative, and concepts that are useful without needing to be applicable. Philosophical writing *weaves* in two senses of the word: joining together (as on a loom) and creating (as in a story). Precisely because of this, it cannot be formalised, and neither does it admit standards or protocols for evaluation and communication.

What are the conditions for the possibility of this writing? It is difficult to say because there is no lab-produced philosophy, but there is a condition that the practice of philosophy has made its own from the very start: teaching. Philosophy was born in teaching and there are hardly any philosophers who have not taught philosophy one way or another and in some kind of relationship with it. Shaw's dictum, adopted by the artistic domain, 'Those who can, do; those who cannot, teach', does not apply to philosophy. The greatest philosophers have made teaching part of their philosophy, whether in institutional or convivial environments, from a mentor–disciple relationship, or opening up spaces for thinking among friends. What is the relationship between teaching and writing as the two elements in which philosophical thinking develops? Can writing be taught? What does this teaching consist of? In what spaces can it occur?

There are ideas, discoveries, inventions, and knowledge that happen in laboratories, in computers, or excavations, and they are communicated in writing to the respective communities of experts and, finally, through popularising publications, to the rest of society. Philosophy does not work like that. It 'happens' through writing. What is going on here is no longer communication and, moreover, everything is going on at once, without stages or interventions. In philosophy, there are no degrees of writing but different ways of approaching it. A book by Nietzsche is a book by Nietzsche, but a student of his thought, a philosopher looking for an interlocutor in Nietzsche, a philosophy enthusiast in general, and an adolescent urgently looking for answers to assuage their painful loneliness will all read him differently. The best philosophy is that which, without holding anything back, offers its writing to all possible approximations, without confusing them but also without creating a hierarchy.

What is this that 'happens' in writing? Primarily, in philosophy, to write is to be transformed. As in Foucault's well-known words, one writes to become other than what one is or, more specifically, 'There is a modification of the way of being that can be glimpsed through the act of writing.'* This transformation affects one's own thinking in the movement of writing: 'The book transforms me and what I think.'† But how does this happen? The self-modifying process takes place through a specific practice of writing that is not confused, though it may overlap with others like poetry or composing music.

---

* Michel Foucault, *Dits et écrits*, vol. 4, 1980–1988, Paris: Gallimard, 1994, p. 605.
† Ibid., p. 41.

What philosophy does is to propose new variations on already existing problems and to create essential concepts for them. Creating concepts is thus an exercise in embodied abstraction. It is not alien to the body of the philosopher who takes it on, or to his or her real-life situation, and yet it goes beyond him or her by means of an appeal to a common way of thinking, to an intelligibility that demands to be addressed. As a result of this, philosophy's 'place of enunciation' cannot be neutral. The person who thinks, who writes, is involved and directly concerned with what he or she needs to think. There is a vital need that thus guides philosophy and dictates its breathing.*

This means that, like discourse, philosophy is necessarily connected with a way of life. Philosophy is a way of speaking that appeals to a way of living, with regard to oneself and also to others. Rectification of names, said Confucius, is reordering the world. This connection has been worked on in many ways throughout history, from the classical idea of the exemplariness of the philosophical life to philosophy's modern call to existential creativity and political transformation of the world. Whatever the case, philosophy is only residually a theory. Theory is what is left of philosophy when it is dissociated and neutralised as a necessary questioning of living (its value, meaning, languages, and so on).†

The value of philosophy as an experience of transformation is not only in the result it might have for oneself but also in

---

* William James, *Essays in Radical Empiricism*, New York: Longmans, Green, and Co., 1912, p. 37: 'The "I think" which Kant said must be able to accompany all my objects, is the "I breathe" which actually does accompany them.'

† Pierre Hadot's studies offer a very good analysis of this process of philosophy's dissociation as discourse and as a way of life, which was already happening in the development of Greek philosophy but especially after the demotion of philosophy to the 'servant' of theology throughout the Middle Ages. See, for example, Pierre Hadot, *What Is Ancient Philosophy?*, trans. Michael Chase, Cambridge, MA: Belknap Press, 2002.

its power of engagement. It has sometimes been asserted that philosophy is the changing formulation of eternal problems. They are not eternal, but they are problems that keep challenging us. So, rather than being immortal, they remain alive, or become alive again, though being transformed, thanks to each act of writing that is able to give them new life.

Writing philosophy, then, is not just about being transformed, but also means opening up a place of encounter and debate. Summaries of the history of philosophy present us with great philosophers according to what they have said, according to what they have stated. It would be interesting to produce a history someday that will tell us what they listened to. There is no philosophy without listening, without reception, without contagion, without insemination. It is not just a matter of how some schools influence others, but of the reception of what remains to be thought in each case. Listening to what has not been thought: only this will free the desire to keep thinking, to write again about what is already been written, and the need to go back or to start again.

Writing as an experience of transformation and place of questioning and debate is, perforce, creative, experimental, bodily, stylistic, and singular writing. 'So, the question of philosophy is the singular point where concept and creation are related to each other', write Deleuze and Guattari in *What Is Philosophy?** What would philosophical writing be if we could not recognise the author's pen in its tone and rhythm, in its own way of getting to the truth? But the author's pen, as Nietzsche aptly puts it, is not an owner's signature but the movement of a body dancing. The steps of the dance are learned, are practised, but in the end each body has its own way of performing them, its own way of giving them life. Even the most austere of philosophical pens, even the most impersonal and anonymous

---

* Gilles Deleuze and Félix Guattari, *What Is Philosophy?*, trans. Hugh Tomlinson and Graham Burchell, New York: Columbia University Press, 1994, p. 11, n14.

writing, has its tone and style if it really has embraced the problem it is tackling and accepted the need to unfold its concepts and be transformed with them. Philosophical styles have changed, not only in accordance with authors, but also times, fashions, political and institutional situations, the traditions of schools, and the means of publishing and distribution of the writing. In each epoch, moreover, writings have lived in tense coexistence and open conflict over the content of their propositions, and also their way of enunciating them.

When writing, in philosophy, becomes a mere means of communicating theories, philosophy stops thinking, transforming us, and challenging us. Learning to think is learning to write. We constitute a society that is fully schooled in the technique of writing. But I fear that we are a society that is threatened with a new kind of illiteracy, which is that of having a merely instrumental relationship with reading and writing. Hence, writing is ceasing to be a means for understanding and expressing personal and collective experience and only to be reduced to a tool of communication.

9

Learning to Think

Thinking is learning to think. This is something that philosophy has proclaimed and practised since it took its very first steps, so it is not an activity that is separable from teaching or learning. The fact that thinking means learning to think entails essentially two things: that, normally, we do not think, and that there is no already accepted way of thinking. The former situates philosophy in a relation of conflict with established opinions and knowledge, and the latter places it in tension with itself, since it does not admit stabilisation, accumulation, and predictability in its ways of thinking. Thinking is learning to think because thinking means thinking again. But then how is it possible to teach? What might be the intrinsic educational sense of a practice of thinking that occurs in the displacement of both established knowledge and its own achievements?

What philosophy as an educational practice proposes is that education is not about acquiring skills, conveying knowledge, or schooling thoughts. It essentially consists in a displacement, a change of place that renews the desire to think, and a commitment to truth. 'It is something to be able to raise our heads but for a moment and see the stream in which we are sunk so deep. We cannot gain even this transitory moment of awakening by our own strength; we must be lifted up – and who are they that will uplift us?'* These are the true educators, the ones who

---

* Friedrich Nietzsche, 'Schopenhauer as Educator', trans. Adrian Collins, available at wikisource.org, note 26.

make us raise our heads. Raising one's head is also beginning to look and ceasing to obey, discovering the world, uncovering its problems as matters that concern us, and delving into them free of all servitude, of whatever kind it may be.

The teacher, in philosophy, does not form or train but instead liberates people from what prevents them from thinking. The true teacher is, in the end, the teacher who frees us from the tutelage of the teacher. Now become a friend, they deliver us to the 'happiness of our solitude'.* This is not a paradox. The relationship between friendship and solitude is the condition for starting to think, to relearn how to see the world by rewriting it. Nietzsche says we cannot raise our heads with our own strength. Counter to all the ideas about natural inspiration or the revealed word, philosophy situates us squarely in the terrain of human interdependence. If we think, it is because something is given to us to think about by someone, a teacher, a friend, or a mediator. As Heidegger noted, in the roots of the words 'think', 'thinking', 'thought', the Old English 'thencan' (to think) and 'thanaan' (to thank) are closely related.† Giving to think is thus not indicating how to think or what to think, just as teaching writing is not about putting into practice methodologies and standards of writing. Giving to think, teaching to write, means suggesting that there is still something left to think, something left to write, and thus to unfinish in a saturated, exhausted world. From this perspective, I understand that to teach philosophy is to leave gaps in one's own gestures and words. Teaching philosophy is an invitation.

---

* This expression was used by Gilles Deleuze in the interviews comprising a French television programme, an eight-hour series of interviews called *Abécédaire* (1988–1989), specifically when, under the heading of the letter P for 'professor' (in two parts), he talks about his years as a teacher. 'Gilles Deleuze's alphabet book: P for Professor part 1', SUB-TIL productions, 21 October 2020, video, youtube.com.

† He analyses the relationship in Martin Heidegger, *What Is Called Thinking?*, trans. Fred D. Wieck and J. Glenn Gray, New York: Harper & Row, 1968, pp. 138–9.

Educating, therefore, is initiating others in this displacement, moving them, shaking them up, and seducing them, tearing them away from what they are and what they think they are, from what they know and think they know. Hence, philosophy's relationship with education is at once violent and fecund. It is violent because it strikes at the roots of what is established. It questions what we are and what we know, what we value and what we aim at. It is fecund because it opens up new relationships, new ways of seeing and speaking, in places where only what existed could be perpetuated. In short, it means new approaches to what makes us live. Philosophy's question about education is not and never has been the pedagogical question about how to teach philosophy but, rather, about how to educate the person, the citizen, humanity. It is therefore a question that affects, challenges, and reformulates the image which, in each epoch and in each context, organises both the space of knowledge and the political space.

Is today's university ready to be the place from which these questions can be formulated and their consequences accepted? It would seem that, for the moment, it is not. While it is making its productive, professional, and curricular structures more flexible so as to adapt better to market requirements, the university, as an institution, shields itself from questions and also stops asking them. In this situation, some writers and teachers condemn the forsaking of culture by the present sectorial-university or entrepreneurial-university, now become a collection of professional schools and centres of technological innovation.* Invoking the humanist ideal of the university as the headquarters and driving force of a society's culture, they perceive in today's transformations the betrayal and dismantling of this culture-based project. But let us not be tricked

---

* See Faustino Oncina Coves, ed., *Filosofía para la universidad, filosofía contra la universidad*, Madrid: Dykinson, 2008, and positions like that of Jordi Llovet, *Adiós a la universidad*, Barcelona: Galaxia Gutenberg, 2011.

by the corporate subjugation of the university into deceiving ourselves with nostalgic imaginings of lost freedoms. The culture-based university was a tool of a Western bourgeoisie that had, in 'culture', one of its main assets and sources of cultural hegemony. When universities began to open up to other social classes, this function was lost. Nowadays, culture, in this sense, does not exist and does not serve anyone. Why should the university be defended unless it is to be turned into a mausoleum?

The problem lies elsewhere. Beyond all humanist melancholy, beyond every defensive and conservationist position, what is at stake is a battle for thinking. How can we ensure that the real questions, the ones that matter to us, that move us to write, to learn, and to transform the societies in which we live, do not die crushed by the weight of profitable but powerless knowledge? From where can we reconstruct the alliance between philosophical interrogation and knowledge? Inside or outside the university?

10

University without Surrender

Where to start thinking again, inside or outside the university? This is the question that arises every time the educational and knowledge institutions shield themselves from questions and submit to being yoked to the production of predictable knowledge. Although they remain active, and even increase their economic and institutional standing, what happens is that it is no longer possible to think in them, and there is less and less to think about. The brain drain then begins, the real brain drain of people who are no longer willing to watch how the desire from which all thinking springs is dying within them.

The 'inside or outside' question has been part of the history of the university, as an institution, as long as it has existed. From the medieval theological university, heretics and scientists escaped. From the still-theological modern university escaped the great philosophers of the seventeenth and eighteenth centuries, from Descartes and Spinoza to the French Republic of Letters. After the consolidation of the German university – built on the foundations of the Enlightenment and idealism and embracing all of German philosophy from Kant to Schelling and Hegel – other philosophers like Schopenhauer, Nietzsche, and Marx also had to make their respective escapes. Now we are at a similar juncture. After the social opening of Western universities from the 1960s to the 1980s, letting in voices, problems, and epistemological and socially diverse practices, for some years we have been witnessing their progressive shutting down.

In fact, we are now faced with a new scholasticism under the guise of an apparently innovative discourse, an appearance of knowledge that only starts from itself and makes of this self-referentiality the basis and the source of legitimacy of its power. This is why today's university not only brings about ruptures and expulsions, but also begets increasing indifference in society. Hence, the need to escape, to grow instead in the wild, has appeared once again. As a clear symptom of this, we are presently seeing the development of numerous self-learning platforms, projects of social, cultural, and political experimentation, writing groups, independent publications, networks, forums, and encounters that, fragile as they may be, have opted to take on the task of learning to think.*

Is the university emptying out? In part, yes. The most creative and open forms of knowledge, the processes of producing the freest and yet most committed knowledge, horizontal and collaborative work practices, and so on, are fleeing from academia. Even writing books, which no longer enjoys formal academic recognition, has become an 'undue' activity. Does this mean we should unilaterally choose to be outside, making a point of this while denying any possibility of life in the university? The answer is a contradictory yes and no. Yes, one must radically opt for being outside, but still must not deny any possibility of life within the university. How can these two apparently contradictory positions be reconciled?

The answer can be found in philosophy itself, in its earliest beginnings. If Socrates is something like father and midwife to philosophy, who are the children of Socrates? Many, probably all of us, still are. But in the Athens immediately after him there were basically two, Plato and Diogenes. Plato was the one who baptised philosophy and invented the Academy. Naked Diogenes, who abhorred the conventions of knowledge and its

---

* I analyse this phenomenon in my article 'Dar que pensar. Sobre la necesidad política de nuevos espacios de aprendizaje', in *El combate del pensamiento*, ed. Espai en Blanc, Barcelona: Bellaterra, 2009.

relations with power, lived in a large earthenware jar (*pithos*), and was famously described by Plato as a 'Socrates gone mad'. Academy and *pithos*, man of prestige and stray dog, organisation of all knowledge into a single body and its destruction at root, education and de-education, reformist political aspiration and subversion, this was the double body with which philosophy took its first steps. In China, a similar tension existed between Confucius, father and systematiser of classical texts and the political institutions of what was to become the empire, and the Taoist masters like Laozi and Zhuangzi, among many others, people in flight, feral, and off-centre with regard to all systematisation and institutionalisation of knowledge.

What is presented throughout history as an alternative, an alternation between two conceptions of the word and knowledge is, in fact, a necessary polarity. Without Diogenes, Plato would be a dead end. Without Plato, Diogenes would have been condemned to oblivion. Academy and *pithos* need one another, without the possibility of making a synthesis of them, overcoming them, or finding a middle ground. On the one hand, knowledge needs to be consolidated and organised, and it must promote contact between different areas of knowledge. On the other hand, the questions addressed by knowledge die if they cease to be exposed to their own limits and the true problems that feed them: the problem of life, its raison d'être, and the ways of living life.

Philosophy's difficult task is to keep alive this remediless tension. But if I am sure of anything, it is that this is the difficulty (and not its supposed founding or systematising nature) that situates philosophy at the basis or root of knowledge. The academic option, trying to be self-sufficient, dies of self-absorption. The feral option, breaking all communication with existing knowledge and social institutions, dissipates into personal stances and private micro-worlds that have no qualms about ceasing to speak to each other. Then again, this 'feral' outside of educational institutions is not a real outside today, but one that is densely structured and dominated by market forces and their corresponding power dynamics, which make it very difficult for thought and creation to survive out in the open.

Against the 'compartments' that 'represent institutional confirmation of the renunciation of the whole truth', denounced by Adorno, and without losing sight of the fact that all forms of thought are mutually supportive and need to be in contact with each other, philosophy's task is to keep this tension alive because only within it can the desire for knowledge and commitment to the truth be renewed.* Philosophy loses its ability to keep this tension alive every time it becomes just another discipline, as in the case of the modern university, when philosophy is assigned a place among the human and social sciences. Its be-wildering virtue thus becomes productive impotence. Its a-topical nature is reduced to meta-discourse or 'transversal competence', as the new methodological terminology would have it. Its writing, slavishly on its knees, is turned into helpless theoretical discourse that refers to other theoretical discourse.

This is a time of growing disconnection between the academic and the feral, and, in it, philosophy as such does not need to be defended or saved from the hounding to which it is subjected as a discipline of the human and social sciences. As a discipline of the human and social sciences, it was stillborn. It needs to be freed from this 'classification' so it can do its job, so it can once again connect established knowledge with its outside, what is thought with what is not thought, knowledge with not-knowledge.

Philosophical writing is that which, from a commitment to truth, connects knowledge with not-knowledge. It is writing that works at the limits of what is known, what is thought, what is established, at the limits of the enunciable and the

---

* Theodor W. Adorno, 'The Essay as Form', in *Notes to Literature*, vol. 1, ed. Rolf Tiedemann, trans. Shierry Weber Nicholsen, New York: Columbia University Press, 1991, p. 7.

recognisable. Philosophical writing elaborates the limits of language itself. It therefore does not submit to the inside/outside blackmail but instead restores the connection over and over again, thus attacking the neutering myth that places a cordon sanitaire between disciplines, between legitimacies, between ways of speaking, between sound and silence, between the thought and the not-thought. As Deleuze and Guattari write, 'If philosophy is paradoxical by nature, this is not because it sides with the least plausible opinion or because it maintains contradictory opinions but rather because it uses sentences of a standard language to express something that does not belong to the order of opinion or even of the proposition.'* Its disturbing nature resides precisely in the undermining of standard language to make it say what does not fit into it. In Heidegger's well-known words, 'Words are wellsprings that are found and dug up in the telling.'†

Against the standardisation of writing and thinking, it is essential, then, to keep writing philosophy, to philosophise by teaching, and to teach to write. Thus understood, philosophy is not humanistic heritage about to starve to death and in danger of extinction, but the most powerful weapon with which the university, itself in danger of asphyxiation, can wield in the fight against becoming a global enterprise for mass production of ultra-specialised professionals and sterile, redundant knowledge.

In 1998, Jacques Derrida gave a lecture titled 'The University Without Condition' at Stanford University, in California, where he proposed that the university *should* be the place of double unconditionality, that of a limitless commitment to truth, and that of absolutely heterogeneous dissidence against any type of power. The university *should* therefore be 'an *unconditional*

---

* Gilles Deleuze and Félix Guattari, *What Is Philosophy?*, trans. Hugh Tomlinson and Graham Burchell, New York: Columbia University Press, 1994, p. 80, n14.

† Ibid., p. 158, n35.

freedom to question and to assert' governed by 'the right to say publicly all that is required by research, knowledge, and thought concerning the *truth*'.* Unconditional freedom, unconditional discussion, unconditional resistance, and unconditional dissidence *should* be manifestations of the 'profession of faith' in truth, which the university would embody. The principle that would govern its justice is thought. Accordingly, Derrida conceives of the university as the privileged place of the philosophical and its future as the promise of a 'new Humanities'. As I have shown, the whole discourse in Derrida's text about the university without condition is conjugated in the conditional. For Derrida, the university without condition situates us in a time of a 'perhaps', on the horizon of a commitment with what is '*de jure*' and in relation to 'an event that, without necessarily coming about tomorrow, would remain perhaps – and I underscore *perhaps* – to come ...'

Contrasting with Derrida's position, there is another proposal of unconditionality: instead of the *should*, a 'must', and instead of a *perhaps*, a 'for the moment', and, instead of a profession of faith in absolute terms regarding the university to come, taking a specific stance in the currently existing university. What does the unconditionality of this position consist of? Opening up spaces of the non-negotiable. Specifically, in terms of what concerns us here, teaching the writing of philosophy in the university is a non-negotiable commitment. Non-negotiable is something that has value in itself, that does not answer to externally imposed calculations. In this case, teaching philosophy writing in the university is a commitment that declares that it breaks with all the measures that justify and evaluate academic activity. It is justified by its own necessity alone.

This necessity is embodied by specific people, each person who comes to the university moved by a desire to learn.

---

* Jacques Derrida, 'The University Without Condition', in *Without Alibi*, ed. and trans. Peggy Kamuf, Stanford, CA: Stanford University Press, 2002, p. 202.

Obviously, the desire to learn is not pure desire, but a desire linked to the need to acquire professional skills and earn a living. Why not? The self-sufficiency of the wise person is an ideal, either aristocratic or religious, and reflects the original elitism of access to knowledge and thought. But today, for humanity as a whole, knowledge and work, learning and money, are perforce intertwined. Without denying this impurity, but enlisting as part of it, the university is the place where two things of the order of the incalculable or the non-negotiable can still happen: taking seriously the desire to know, for its own sake; and learning that this knowledge 'is not enough'. In other words, all knowledge implies non-knowledge, and all knowledge appeals to a way of life that has personal, social, and political consequences that go beyond its specificity. This is the non-philosophical task that cannot be negotiated in the presently existing university.

Proposing a university without surrender is not, to my mind, a call to redouble our efforts to defend the university. Rather, it is a commitment not to surrender *to it*, not to surrender *in it*. 'But this is precisely where culture begins – namely, in understanding how to treat the quick as something vital.'* The university may be more dead than alive, but we, each one of us who teaches and studies in it, are among the quick and not the dead, and we must treat each other as being alive. I cautiously situate at the centre of this position-taking, a 'for the moment'. It is possible that the asphyxia of thought in the university will come to such a pass that, someday, this position-taking will cease to make sense. We will need to be attentive to this possibility and know how to make the right decisions when we need to. So, not surrendering to the university also entails not failing to nourish what is happening outside the university, what escapes, what does not fit, what can only be done and

---

* Friedrich Nietzsche, *On the Future of Our Educational Institutions: Homer and Classical Philology*, trans. J. M. Kennedy, Edinburgh: T. N. Foulis, 1909, p. 50.

tested outside the institutional frameworks we know. Maybe these trials, these attempts will, in the future, give us pointers on how to move beyond the university itself.

The question about the place of philosophy in higher education today, formulated by means of analysing the standardisation of writing and the possibilities of teaching philosophy in today's universities, brings us to the need to open up spaces of the non-negotiable in the university, to maintain them and experiment with them, as a commitment that concerns all of us who, whatever our field of knowledge, are fighting against the asphyxiation of thought in educational, creative, and research practice.

11

The New Alliances

The problem of standardisation of thought in the academic domain has opened up the question about whether the place for philosophical thinking is inside or outside the university. It leads, once again, to the question about limits and the need to think differently. As with the question about the national and cultural places of philosophy, we have moved towards the fringes, frontiers, and transit zones. And we have met with philosophy itself as a frontier that joins the philosophical and the non-philosophical, the academic and the feral, knowing and not-knowing, in accordance with relationships and problems that are not predetermined. This is what the standardisation of thought fences in and neutralises. Defending philosophy cannot take the form of entrenchment in these cordoned-off territories in competition with other disciplines, as has sometimes been proclaimed, somewhat dramatically. On the contrary. It means undertaking a movement of opening up and challenging, of dissemination and alliances, a guerrilla philosophy, one against purism and disciplinary isolation.

This challenge inevitably raises another crucial problem for me, namely that of the unity of knowledge. Criticism of unitary systems of thought and the automatisation processes with particular sciences had left this question locked away in a back room, like an old ghost. But I think the present situation requires bringing up the question again, without fear of reviving old dangers. What is the relationship between the present sciences and forms of knowledge and wisdom? And what relationship can we establish between the different domains of experience, between theory and practice, and between thought and life?

These questions become urgent at a time like ours when the academic and media proliferation of knowledge – without in any way helping us to make sense of experience – is threatening our societies with new forms of illiteracy, as I have already described. This is the illiteracy of a civilisation that is threatened by the saturation of information and segmentation of knowledge. Despite the general population's high levels of education and more or less free access to a whole range of knowledge that was unthinkable not so long ago, the new illiteracy is the experience of being unable to have an autonomous and meaningful relationship with such information and forms of knowledge. It is a knowledge that breeds dependence and, therefore, submission.

Saturation of information and stimuli inhibits attention and inhibits the consequences of paying attention. As many of us know from everyday experience, our attention is literally neutralised by the bombardment of information to which it is subjected and is rendered unable to relate to what is being asked of it. And there is more to it than that. Not only are we unable to relate to everything that comes to us but, since we know that there is even more of the same out there waiting for us, it is increasingly difficult for us to set out our own desires and needs and chart the paths we want to explore. How can we sense what we lack and what we need to know when we are already overwhelmed by what is already there waiting for us? And how can we forge free relationships between items that are pre-packaged by title, novelty, most recent publication, portfolios, showcases, and bulletins that are constantly being updated?

Moreover, all this information and its corresponding packets of knowledge are increasingly segmented in their presentation. It has been quite a while now since the first warnings were issued against specialisation. The development in modernity of the sciences and technologies led to growing difficulty in the various disciplines and autonomy among themselves as well as with their common core of philosophy. The result was the appearance of a new kind of ignorance, the one all of us inevitably suffer from today: that of only knowing about one discipline and radically ignoring even the most basic notions of others. This tendency was somewhat slowed until the middle of the twentieth century with the idea of a general culture which acted as container and sounding board for the different scientific, artistic, and humanistic specialties, but nowadays even this notion has become unviable.

The question that arises, then, is whether we have all become specialists and only specialists. The answer is that this is not the case either. Increasingly complex and demanding, true specialisation is the realm of very few, while what is produced in general is segmentation of knowledge and audiences, in both the market and in academia. We are offered knowledge and technological and cultural products in keeping with segments, by age, income, origins, and so on. The segment is not a fragment. There has been much debate in postmodernity about the value of the fragment in the end times of grand narratives and systems. The fragment is ambivalent, at once ruinous and free: something broken and something freed to open up a field of uncertainty and the possibility of new relations. The segment, by contrast, is a construction that classifies, guides, and organises the reception of knowledge, determining distance in order to manage in ways that are predictable and identifiable.

Given the new illiteracy caused by the segmentation of knowledge and information overload, the question about the unity of knowledge raises the need to establish, now, new relationships and levels of experience. In 1998, the American biologist Edward O. Wilson published *Consilience: The Unity of Knowledge*, in which he suggests that the confluence of different branches of knowledge, not only in the sciences and

humanities but also in ethics, religion, and politics, is a necessary and inevitable process.* Without proposing a systematic
and formal unification, externally constructed by something
like professional philosophers, Wilson shows that the problems of our own times, for which no particular science has an
answer, require such tools and developments. The keys of these
problems are to be found at the two opposite poles that have
organised human experience: the self and the world. Today,
the self is a phenomenon that, far from being lauded as the
sovereign identity of consciousness, appears as the effect of
cerebral processes that are difficult to delimit in their material
and symbolic scope. From what we are starting to learn about
the brain today, where does the self begin and where does it
end? How many dimensions comprise it? From what biological and cultural, genetic, and social processes is it generated at
any given moment? Today, neither the shepherds of souls, nor
philosophers of the mind, nor social psychologists, nor neuro-
biologists have the last word on the self, consciousness, or
personal identity as the basic focus on which our relationship
with the world and with others is established and sustained.

The world, on the other hand, is a set of complex ecosystems
in which it is no longer possible to separate nature and society,
animality and humanity, and the inside and outside of territories inhabited by humans. From the infinite universe to the
exhausted planet, and in between, there is an immense set of
variables that no science can reduce and systematise on its own.
The relationship with the environment, with what surrounds
us, can no longer be said to be merely contemplative, and its
capacity for influence cannot be restricted to certain aspects of
reality. Any observation is now involved in decisions and found
to be caught up in a chain of consequences that overflow the
frameworks of its own conceptual structure.

---

* E. O. Wilson, *Consilience: The Unity of Knowledge*, New York:
Vintage, 1999.

The alliance between knowledge and decisions is today therefore announced as necessary. It is an overflow that brings down barriers because of the need to respond to shared problems. From this position, Wilson argues that we need to get past the war between cultures, between these 'two cultures', of science and letters – which C. P. Snow wrote about in 1959 – a war that has so artificially organised the thoroughgoing mutilation of our learning and our experience of the world, even in educational programmes from a very early age. When referring to overcoming this confrontation, Wilson also resorts to the image of the frontier and suggests that we should stop thinking about it as a territorial boundary and instead regard it as a vast, uncharted territory that now requires joint exploration by both parties.

This same cultural, epistemological, and political situation is what Ilya Prigogine and Isabelle Stengers explore in their well-known book *Order Out of Chaos: Man's New Dialogue with Nature* (first published in French in 1978), taking the evolution of physics as their starting point.[*] The interesting thing about this book, as in Wilson's, is that the alliance between science and culture is not presented as an ideal or a plea. It is shown as the inevitable situation resulting from the evolution of sciences that have atomised and attempted to establish themselves as hegemonic. This is the case of physics, which tried to be a universal language. Going back over the evolution of modern physics, Prigogine and Stengers demonstrate that the founding assumption of classical science has been surpassed. This was based on the premise of a threefold isolation, of man in the universe, of science in culture, and of the scientific community in society. With the development of physics throughout the twentieth century, humankind rediscovered the situated and thus involved nature of its relationship with its milieu and the quest for truth. Hence, science is also re-encountering its

* Ilya Prigogine and Isabelle Stengers, *Order Out of Chaos: Man's New Dialogue with Nature*, London: Verso, 2018.

relations with other ways of thinking and looking, and is once again situated as a cultural complex starting from which each generation of humanity tries to find a form of intellectual coherence.

This new alliance, or new continuity, between science, culture, and nature, enables Prigogine and Stengers to speak of a re-enchantment with the world. This is not a backswing of the pendulum from the Enlightenment to the mythical, or from the rational to the irrational. It is about rediscovering the possibility of speaking about the world from the powers of imagination and experimentation without being subjected to what they call the Kantian critique. Kant brought about a break that struck at the root of the modern experience of the world when, with no possible mediation, he separated nature and morality, which is to say, rationality with which we can relate to what we have, or what there is, and the rationality that is related with what must be. Starting from an analysis of a priori categories, which is to say considering them independently of all empirical experience, Kant set aside the natural sciences, which were closely scrutinised by the critique of pure reason. On the other side was the moral decision and its more or less approximate historical and political expression. In the middle there was nothing. Or nothing we can say anything meaningful about. And, on the horizon, were art and religion guiding yearnings and encounters that are impossible to systematise.

Prigogine and Stengers invite their readers to take a leap beyond the Kantian critique in company with the most recent science. And, oddly enough, the people they find are neither mystics nor priests but radically enlightened and rationalist thinkers and writers like Diderot, father inter alia of the *Encyclopédie* and of the European materialist enlightenment. I can only enthusiastically support this quick mention by Prigogine and Stengers of Diderot as a clue to be followed up. Diderot is a key figure when thinking about what we might be asked to respond to today by the new alliances between the different branches of knowledge and culture, theory, and practice, and among the various domains of experience. His thought runs across scientific, artistic, and literary practices. He is a man of his times and yet timeless, making a living from his work as an encyclopaedist while also going beyond the bounds of his profession with his philosophical work and his practice of cultural and political agitation. The unity of the various areas of knowledge of his times becomes, for him, a living practice, one that is about searching and experimentation, formalisation and imagination, conjecture and verification. At the same time, his voice is of a plurality bordering on plagiarism. Diderot is a receiver and also a versionist of scientific treatises, of moralist works, of literary inventions, and of the philosophical challenges of an epoch in which thinking for oneself in no way contradicted the need to think with others.

Diderot's thinking is singular and collective, unitary and fragmented, and at once encyclopaedic and unfinished. His radical enlightenment prefigures what might today be an intellectuality that is committed to the shared problems of the times and also of humanity's past and future destiny. Unlike the 'universal man' who brought about the scientific revolution in the Renaissance and the rationalisation of science in the seventeenth century, Diderot is thus a kind of patchwork who, however, does not lose the sense of unity and relationship between knowledge and its consequences. He knows that he cannot know everything, as Descartes, Leibnitz, and Spinoza still seem to be trying to do. His mind can no longer hold the keys of the universal language, and neither is his life as a thinker-worker sufficient to reorder the totality. The *Encyclopédie*, which could try to be a new version based on this same claim, is a great manual of knowledge that is known to be in process and in transformation, beginning with artisanship and then moving on to describe the most innovative theoretical knowledge and cultural discoveries of the time. It is more a state of affairs than a *mathesis universalis*. And Diderot, out of step and ill-adjusted, with himself as both character and alter ego – Rameau's nephew – is someone who makes of the cultural and political centre that is Paris a zone of transit, a place of chiaroscuro for wandering around in and meeting up with what is not visible or thinkable, a margin that is in no way marginal. Diderot empties the centres of power to re-signify the places of knowledge, thence to confer on them a new sense of unity.

The Diderot clue suggests that speaking of new alliances today also means speaking of old wounds, looking for the excisions and expulsions on the basis of which theory has been constituted as a self-sufficient and dominant language. I mentioned the Kantian critique and the way that such judgement split the experience that humans might have of the world into the two radically different spheres of knowledge of nature and moral decision. But at the end of the day, we could also go back to the foundational moments of this split, for example, the Aristotelean distinction between *theoria, poesis,* and *praxis,* or to the expulsion and condemnation of poets, artists, and the people of the theatre in Plato's *The Republic,* and the subordination therein of all productive and reproductive labour. I cannot go into any detailed analysis of these complex references here, but it is important to note that theory, as an activity that seeks to attain a privileged relationship with truth, stood apart from and opposed other ways of being, doing things, and speaking in the world.

Poesis and *praxis* were left at the fringes of theoretical activity because their aims are not within themselves but in some form of productive or creative work or action with consequences. Theory, by contrast, proclaims its free relationship with the truth, establishing as a criterion that this is an end in itself and cannot be subordinated to any other interest or influence. Philosophy is an invitation, then, to think for oneself, without conditions, or with no other condition than this freedom. But this condition ends up becoming a sentence when theoretical discourse is removed from its relationships with practice, creation, and transformation of life and the world. As the works of Pierre Hadot have so well shown, the shaping of ways of life and elaboration of theoretical and scientific discourse are two heterogeneous but inseparable dimensions that refer to the same radical choice, which is to set out autonomously, without guarantees or prejudices, in search of the truth. Their separation is their neutralisation. Ways of life become lifestyles, and discourses become sterile theoretical products. Likewise, numerous philological, anthropological, philosophical, and historical studies now show the heterogeneous continuity of, and not the excluding opposition between, myth and *logos*, between the mysterious enigma and the philosophical problem, poetry and rational discourse, metaphor and concept, manual work and ways of thinking, productive challenges and rational categories.

Once again, we are on liminal ground crossed through with relationships in tension but not on a frontier between oppositions. Considering the inevitable unity of knowledge today means daring to explore these borderlands, digging into old wounds, and experimenting with new alliances, always with our attention open to what the problems of our times require us to think about, even if we do not know how or from whence to do this.

12

End of the 'Great Men'

The terrain of the new alliances blurs the figure of the philosopher. I am writing about him as masculine because he is an eminently male figure, even today. In Western culture, the philosopher has been a character that moves between heroism and ridiculousness, grandeur and weirdness, majesty and ugliness, admiration and mockery. He has played all the extravagant roles but none in the middle ground of normality.

Not much is said about the private lives of philosophers, though it is known that their whole life is at stake in the decision to lead a philosophical existence, which explains their detachment from private interests and disdain for practical goals. Throughout history, it is not unusual for philosophers to be childless and nowadays, for example, not know how to drive. But it is from this very radicalness of existential choice that their commitment to humanity and its destiny derives. The philosopher's life is a particular one that is devoted to a universal problem, a singular voice in search of a shared reasoning. This means vocation, schooling in wide-ranging and difficult knowledge, and, in many cases, personal risk. Since the death of Socrates, which is the foundational myth of Western philosophy, there have been stories of political persecution, personal and social non-adaptation, physical disorders and mental unbalance, which make philosophy a risky activity. In our culture, it all means that philosophers have been seen as a strange species of great men. Always men, more or less well-off, or at least economically protected, the great men of philosophy radiate a halo that seems to shine even today when their names are uttered.

However, over the last two centuries, this image of the philosopher has been changing. In a first stage, from the nineteenth to the mid-twentieth century, the philosopher, professionalised or 'professorised', came to be just one more member of disciplined, bureaucratised academic life, and incorporated as an intellectual into the public sphere, which is to say, into the mass media. In Edmund Husserl's famous words, the philosopher is now a functionary of mankind. But, as Agnes Heller counters, philosophy then becomes a professionalised, innocuous form of knowledge that must 'fight for its own dangerousness'.* In recognised academic existence and with the blessing of media presence, the philosopher comes to be a regular figure of the intelligentsia, especially in Europe and its scientific, media, and cultural institutions. This is the bourgeois version of the 'great man', who keeps being the one with a privileged voice and recognition associated with his training and public presence.

Nowadays this intellectuality has lost its status. The public sphere has exploded into thousands of channels of communication that have shattered worlds and references. Neither is there any longer a clear idea of 'general culture' or aspiration for knowledge in the battle for truth. Who do today's intellectuals speak for? How influential are they? What is their social status? There are many phenomena that converge in the distortion of the figure of the intellectual, but it is beyond my scope here to embark on an analysis of these figures in all their complexity. In the specific case of philosophy, there are some processes that greatly complicate identification of this figure and its elevation to the pantheon of great men. They complicate it but also open it up to new possibilities for understanding the practice of thinking in all its radicalness. Basically, three phenomena need to be considered. The feminisation of thinking;

---

* Agnes Heller, *A Radical Philosophy*, Oxford: Basil Blackwell, 1984 [1978], p. 23.

the precaritisation and proletarianisation of academic and cultural work; and the collectivisation of knowledge.

The first of these three factors is the most obvious: women have irrupted into all spheres of professional, political, and cultural life. It was not so many years ago that people were still saying that for a woman to do this she had to become a man. Now they are talking about the feminisation of politics and professions like scientific research and medicine. But can we talk about a feminisation of philosophy? Curiously, women's presence in academic philosophy is less strong than in any of the other areas of study in the humanities, especially among teachers. Philosophy is still very much a male preserve, to the point that it does not align with what is expected in terms of other educational and academic parameters. At most, specifically female academic lines are opened up, namely those that deal with supposedly 'women's' problems, among them gender issues, women's philosophy, and corporeality, and, from the traditional fields, ethics.

Gender studies, also called feminist studies, are evidently a conquest but they often function as an annex to the temple of pure philosophy of great concerns, where some men want to continue as high priests. But cracks in the temple appeared long ago. Winds blow and problems change. If women can and want to do philosophy, then philosophy itself has to change and, although it is barely perceptible, this is what is starting to happen. Men and women are working in a more tentative, receptive, and collaborative process of thinking. In their 'Geophilosophy' chapter, Deleuze and Guattari speak of friendship and rivalry as the two conditions for the appearance, in Greece, of philosophical thinking. When men and women come together in the arena of friendships and rivalries, many parameters of these relationships begin to change because their dimensions are multiplied. We must not fall into the temptation of dualising the masculine and feminine of thought and setting them in opposition. But in fact, we women have been historically associated with dimensions of personal and collective life which, until now, have been excluded from what has been conceptually thinkable. With the emergence of women on the philosophical stage, these questions challenge us all and demand a shared philosophical approach. The contours and modes of philosophy are thus beginning to slide into traditionally ignored and despised terrains. It is not just a matter of repairs. What is at stake is a true transformation of philosophy itself.

The first phenomenon, the feminisation of philosophy, is closely linked with the second, which is to say its proletarisation or precaritisation. As is well known in other professional fields, when an activity is downgraded, the presence of women in it increases. Primary care medicine is a recent case, preceded some time ago by primary education, now basically staffed by women teachers. A professional career in philosophy, in secondary and university teaching, once relatively privileged work, is now becoming precarious as it is seen as an unprofitable sector and thus on the way to being dispensable. The professional philosopher is then becoming one more precarious figure in the academic and cultural world, a worker who must develop multiple skills, agree to countless commitments, cultivate an agenda of contacts, and do piecework in accordance with deadlines, schedules, and teaching commitments. The impact of precaritisation on one's life is devastating in many aspects. But what are the consequences for philosophy itself in the ways conceptual thought can be carried out and shared today?

On the one hand, the self-sufficiency and systematicity of the work, as the product of the thinker, is radically called into question. The work is scattered into a multitude of interventions, of formats and registers, that are difficult to organise under the classical concept of a 'work' in the sense of opus. More than a production with clear boundaries, the 'work' becomes a working-through of very different territories, so that the limits between philosophy and non-philosophy inevitably chafe against each other. Pure philosophy becomes contaminated. At risk of becoming prologue writing or commentary on some or other kind of cultural activity, it also has the possibility of going to look for shared problems that really need to be thought about.

On the other hand, not only the self-sufficiency of philosophy but also that of philosophers, whose way of life, as a form of a radical choice, places them at the bounds of practical aims and private interests, is radically challenged. Although the Greek experience of philosophy was born in the streets as an art of dialogue in public spaces, it also appeared as an elitist phenomenon because of its detachment from the world of labour. This disengagement later became an existence free from need because it was protected by political, religious, and academic institutions. What happens when someone who is making a career as a philosopher experiences material need and thus shares this dependent position with his fellow humans? It was Diderot who beautifully portrayed the philosopher's misgivings about this shared condition of need. In his philosophical drama *Rameau's Nephew*, he presents an unattached philosopher strolling alone in a Paris park, following the dictates of his ideas, his only loves. In this carefree, aimless wandering, he meets the nephew of the great musician Rameau, a loathsome man who fills his stomach by playing the buffoon at the tables of the rich, pandering to their craving for culture, extravagance, and excitement. By comparison, the philosopher displays his model of virtue and self-sufficiency. But Rameau disturbs him, and eventually exposes him. Neither is he, the philosopher, a non-participant in the great dance of the scum of the earth, wriggling around like grubs to join the feast. Under his trappings of nobility is a body that is as hungry as any other, as exposed to disease and need for care, and as fearful and exposed to danger as any other mortal. Only the fiction arising from material well-being can be translated into an idea of a life free of needs. The present increasingly precarious condition of people who work as philosophers destroys this mirage. The (so to speak) proletarianisation of the philosopher heralds a turn towards thinking from need and from alliances with other kinds of knowledge and interests that, discounted as lowly, had traditionally been excluded from the philosophical citadel.

Finally, this brings us to the third phenomenon that is altering the maps of knowledge and, with them, those of philosophy: the collectivisation of knowledge. By definition, knowledge has always been a collective fact, but, inasmuch as certain kinds of knowledge could be accumulated and dominated by a single person, it has also been individualised and privatised. With the present bulk, difficulty, and interrelatedness of knowledge, knowing necessarily means that you start out from the fact that you only know a small part of each area of knowledge, whatever the type may be; that you can only know something as an extension of the knowledge of others; that you can only engage in new practices and make new discoveries by cooperating with what others are doing. This raises the debate about forms of cooperation and their effects on recognition and authorship. It pits patenting against sharing, and corporative cooperation against free cooperation. In the case of philosophy, this encounter appears to be rather skewed because cooperation is never able to completely cancel out the uniqueness of the philosophical voice and the experience of life behind it. I said before that philosophy is the expression of a singular voice in search of shared reasoning. What is at stake today is the meaning of this singularity and of this commonality. And what is being opened up is the possibility of understanding them in alliance. The singularity of a person's own voice and own experience does not annul anything but presupposes the realm of what is shared. The philosophy of an individual can hardly aspire to the totality of a system of thought, but this does not mean that the partiality of this person's perspective on the world is condemned to either relativism or irrelevance. It is our job today to work on what I would call an open-source philosophy which knows it is partial, provisional, and furthered by other viewpoints and other variations. It is unfinished, then, but still radical.

Women, precarity, and shared knowledge: philosophy seems to have been stripped of grandeur. It is the end of the great men. The Russian philosopher Boris Groys speaks of the philosophical readymade as the material that present-day philosophy can work with. He therefore calls it antiphilosophy.* Apparently in crisis, unable to rise to its own ideals, this is a philosophy that is able to start touching what is ugly, what is broken, what is specific, what is necessary in the world around us, in the reality of what we are and so determined to deny. The what we can think is inseparable from who can think. Cracks are opening up in the aristocratic airs of pure philosophy and, slipping through them, philosophy's egalitarian vocation, the premise that we are all equipped for thinking, could become a reality.

---

* Boris Groys, *Introduction to Antiphilosophy*, London: Verso, 2012.

13

Body and Thought

The experience of need is anchored in the body, and we are bound to it. The battle from the body and against the body has thus been one of philosophy's key questions. This is not just one issue among many. The battle to go beyond the limits of the body might somehow be philosophy itself.

If the twentieth century was that of philosophy's linguistic turn, we could say that the twenty-first century is that of its somatic turn. Does this mean that it is one of reconciliation with the dimension of ourselves that a culture focused on the soul had denied and scorned? In part, yes. But it would be an oversimplification to see this as a re-encounter between two opposing parties. It is more like an inquiry into and a critique of the way we have become a single but divided entity, one in an irreconcilable reality and in conflict. Aspiring to a shared reasoning, equally accessible to all consciousness, philosophy comes up against the singularity, deformity, partiality, and need of bodies. And bodies are multiple and plural, uncertain and deceitful. They do not admit a possible synthesis of their points of view. What truth can come out of this unyielding plurality of bodies? This is why philosophy projects itself into a beyond and presents itself as the path to go outside and against the body's limits.

The famous Platonic images and stories appeal to this need to move beyond the topology of the body and take a path leading out. Taking up anew religious and mystical experiences, this path is understood as a way to liberation. Yet, this liberation is no longer in the domain of the sacred experience but instead in the flow of reason beyond the walls of the cave of the senses, of the prison of one's own body. This philosophical liberation has a twofold effect: becoming aware of one's state of enslavement, and that of the discovery, for oneself, of the escape route into the light that is waiting to be discovered. Despite the ideological slant that Christian Platonism would later take, in Plato there is no sin or guilt in the body. There is error, pain, partiality, difference, finitude. And philosophy is a human tool for overcoming them.

The other important expression of philosophical dualism can be found in the writings of Descartes in his modern effort to free us from dogmatism by means of clear, distinct ideas. He also necessarily comes up against the variegated effects of a body that does not neatly distinguish between the true and deceptive data that come to it through the senses, that has non-verifiable perceptions of itself, like pain, and that loses its bearings in the confused terrains of sleep and wakefulness. Descartes wonders what to do with all this when trying to recompose a free and yet solid relationship with the knowledge we can have of the world and about ourselves. He then does what he does best. He distinguishes and separates.

> Simply by knowing that I exist and seeing at the same time that absolutely nothing else belongs to my nature or essence except that I am a thinking thing, I can infer correctly that my essence consists solely in the fact that I am a thinking thing. It is true that I may have ... a body that is very closely joined to me. But nevertheless, on the one hand I have a clear and distinct idea of myself, in so far as I am simply a thinking, non-extended thing; and on the other hand I have a distinct idea of body, in so far as this is simply an extended, non-thinking thing. And accordingly, it is certain that I am really distinct from my body, and can exist without it.*

* René Descartes, 'Sixth Meditation: The Existence of Material

For Descartes, the body is the part of me that occupies a space but does not think. More than a way to liberation, philosophy is now a tool for discrimination and clarification. Its precise, methodological use is helpful and necessary for putting the body in its place and thus avoiding confusion. The philosophy of great men has therefore endeavoured to abandon the body and put it in its place. The body does not only deceive us with its senses and its passions. Also and above all, it inescapably binds us to work, reproduction, illness, and death. The body is, in the last instance, the corpse, the body finally present, the complete and finished presence of itself. It is in order to escape from this implacable presence that the body, in despair over itself, has invented an afterlife. It projects an illusion beyond itself and more than an expression of longing, it is one of contempt for and terror it feels of itself. Foucault says, following Nietzsche, Diderot, Merleau-Ponty, and maybe also Lucretius and the ancient materialists, that utopias were born from the body and rose up against it. Against gravity, lightness of thought. Against need, freedom. Against finitude, eternity. Against partiality, universality. Against localisation, utopia. Against my body, my self. But this I, writes Nietzsche in *Thus Spoke Zarathustra*, 'this most honest being, this ego – it speaks of love and it still wants the body, even when it poetizes and fantasizes and flutters with broken wings.'* Lightness, freedom, eternity, universality, utopia, and subjectivity over the powers of thought, and against the impotence of the body. But this confrontation is what the body invents as a body or, rather, it is what it spits out as a residual object. The body, despairing of itself, invents the soul, and the soul spits out the

---

Things and the Real Distinction between Mind and Body', in *Meditations on First Philosophy*, ed. and trans. John Cottingham, rev. ed., Cambridge: Cambridge University Press, 1996.

    * Friedrich Nietzsche, *Thus Spoke Zarathustra*, ed. Adrian Del Caro and Robert Pippin, trans. Adrian Del Caro, Cambridge: Cambridge University Press, 2006, p. 21.

body reduced to an object that can be dominated, calculated, managed. Domesticated and, in the end, buried.

But what is rejected returns and protests. And the body has never stopped protesting. Nietzsche remarks that 'there is more reason in your body than in your best wisdom', and asks: 'What are these leaps and flights of thought to me?'* With this question, he rebels against his condition of object, of machine, of prison, and of shroud. He has offered to us as the set of relations that are I, my self. I am my body, Merleau-Ponty proclaimed as the beginning of a new philosophy that closes Cartesian clarity with a new visibility in which the body is no longer an object confronting a subject. The body is no longer that which is there, binding us to the place, but the condition for every place. It is the ground zero of all spatialities from which we can gain experience and, at the same time, of all the ties that constitute us, materially and psychically. In his lecture 'Utopian Body', Foucault says, 'My body is like the City of the Sun. It has no place, but it is from it that all possible places, real or utopian, emerge and radiate.'† Hence, it is not in space but is space itself, in its many scales and dimensions. But then, who am I, and how do I know that I am myself? If the body is not the object of a subject but a complex set of relations in continuity with other realities, where do the unity and singularity that make it possible to experience each body as unique and different reside?

Diderot asks these questions very radically and amusingly in his *Conversation between D'Alembert and Diderot* (1769), an absurdist yet well-documented dialogue in which his friend D'Alembert speaks with his lover about the advances in and consequences of biological science for the moment between dreams. Who speaks between dreams? Is it D'Alembert himself?

---

* Ibid., p. 23.

† Michel Foucault, 'Utopian Body', in *Sensorium: Embodied Experience, Technology, and Contemporary Art*, ed. Caroline A. Jones, Cambridge, MA: MIT Press, 2006, p. 233.

Descartes would say it is not. But Diderot situates us on the threshold of the self, where we do not know if we are or if we are not ourselves. Who dreams our dreams? Who thinks our thoughts? Diderot says something more or less to this effect: my self, in the end, is nothing but the place to which I most often return. The self is therefore the effect of a return-trip relationship, of a referral of experiences to a shared place that is not a locatable place. Present advances in neuroscience are not very far from Diderot's scientific-poetic conjectures. The brain is seen as a set of scenarios that refer to each other in continuity with the rest of the body and without a central setting.

When the body is not reduced to an object, it is no longer possible to think only of the body, but we can learn to think from the body that we are. There is no need, then, to project an illusion into a beyond. We need to understand that we are an open conjunction of 'more beyonds'. Consequently, lightness and utopia are not opposites of corporality. And the powers of thought acquire other meanings: universality becomes perspectivism or, in other words, the impossible-to-synthesise relationship of all the visions of the world from each one of the bodies that we are. Eternity is not the timelessness of the immutable but the continuity of what is endlessly metamorphosing. And freedom is not set in opposition to need but is understood as the possibility of appropriating and transforming the links that constitute us.

Power and impotence join ranks in a conception of ourselves where appreciation replaces contempt and trust, suspicion. But, meanwhile, our tools of self-criticism and of our possibilities in life become honed. Need, illness, work, reproduction, death, and also the senses and passions, are no longer condemnations to be overcome but realities with which we think of ourselves and the conditions in which this 'we' becomes historically, socially, and politically specific. The path to liberation is no longer that of saving the soul in the light of reason but that of the transformation and improvement of the conditions of life of the vulnerable species that we are. Philosophy is driven by questions about the good life, about the *buen vivir*, as some Indigenous people of Latin America say. Philosophy assumes that this is a question that cannot be answered except by going over and examining together the quest for truths that we can use as criteria for improvement. Today's philosophy, this philosophy in which women, the precariat, and disdained knowledge are all working together, is not afraid of taking these routes at ground level or, as Pessoa said, of brushing against everything that we must experience. If body and thought are not opposed but are intertwined and continue each other, sky and earth, the high and the low, are the two dimensions that meet in this place without a place, in this fragile ground zero that is ours to appear in. And disappear.

From Suspicion to Trust

Thought is suspicious of language. Philosophy begins from a relationship of suspicion of what words let us say, live, and think. That language does not say exactly what it is saying, that it sets traps for us, and that it goes beyond its verbal form because it is limited, are three faces of a suspicion that mobilises the search for truth at the limits of language itself. Forcing, mauling, and submitting our words and speech to the test, probing the conditions for the possibility of their rightness, and creating new meanings and displacements is what philosophy does and has not ceased to do. This is common to the West but also to what we call Eastern philosophies, which have developed their own ways of ensuring that experience of the world does not get stuck behind the bars of language when language becomes autonomous and unable to move with the coming into being of reality.

Wittgenstein's dictum that the limits of my world are the limits of my language is not entirely true, and he himself was later obliged to reconsider. The systems for interpreting the world that organise every social and cultural context are many and changing. If we take all of them together, the limits of the world and of language are then blurry, unstable, and unfinished. There, in this hazy, dangerous border zone, is where philosophy makes sense, where it performs its specific task.

If thinking philosophically is suspecting language, does this mean that philosophy is only an art of suspicion? In 1965, Paul Ricoeur pronounced his famous invocation of Nietzsche,

Freud, and Marx as the 'masters of suspicion', and fathers of contemporary philosophy.* In their shared anti-Cartesian approach, all three would have come to suspect (epistemologically, psychologically, and in class terms) consciousness as a place of clarity and certainty, as a transparent space to go to when searching for the truth. After that, philosophy was to move in the darkness of a muted and fathomless war coinciding with the fact of the death of God and the father. In this battle of powers, God dies, and man loses his autonomy. At bottom, in its sovereignty, the modern Cartesian-style and even Kantian subject still depended on God. Ricoeur, from his explicit Protestant Christianity, tries at the end of this work to find a philosophical reading for this atheist pummelling. He attempts a hermeneutic approximation to this assassination, which would keep hope alive without going back to locking the conquered field of freedom – a freedom liberated from icons but able to save symbols – into a theological-metaphysical system.

Shortly before this, in 1964, Foucault gave a lecture titled 'Nietzsche, Marx, Freud'.† He referred to the three philosophers, who were not yet known as the 'masters of suspicion', situating them as the origin of a thoroughgoing change in the system of interpretations of modernity. For Foucault, Nietzsche, Marx, and Freud are continuers of the stance of suspicion that mobilises our whole philosophical tradition, but they also introduce a leap in scale which is, at the same time, a radical philosophical change. With them, interpretation becomes infinite, always unfinished. 'The incompleteness

---

* Paul Ricoeur, *Freud and Philosophy: An Essay on Interpretation*, trans. Denis Savage, New Haven, CT: Yale University Press, 1970 [1965]; and Paul Ricoeur, *The Conflict of Interpretations: Essays in Hermeneutics*, ed. Don Ihde, Evanston, IL: Northwestern University Press, 1974 [1969].

† Michel Foucault, 'Nietzsche, Marx, Freud', in *Aesthetics, Methods and Epistemology: The Essential Works of Michel Foucault 1954–1984*, vol. 2, ed. James D. Faubion, New York: New Press, 1998, pp. 269–78.

of interpretation, the fact that it is always lacerated and that it remains suspended on its own brink, is found once again, I believe, in a somewhat analogous fashion in Marx, Nietzsche, and Freud in the form of the refusal of beginning." So, despite Ricoeur's felicitous formulation, the question is not suspicion. What introduces a far-reaching change of direction in modern philosophy is this extending the need for interpretation to the infinite and, even in a circular way, to interpretation itself, because there is no first term, no origin, no something to be interpreted that is outside interpretation. What they discover is the irreducible openness of meaning. They peel away all the skins, like layers of an onion, and there is nothing underneath, no God, no first substance, no subject. There is only the intention and the need to keep peeling away the layers. Who has this need and why? What moves this desire? And what cultural, social, and psychic effects does it have? These are the questions of the kind of philosophy where suspicion as a philosophical stance becomes an invitation to interpretation beyond what all the evidence about ourselves would seem to recommend, and beyond what modern pretensions of sovereignty of the subject and its consciousness would seem to indicate.

With Foucault's presentation of Marx, Nietzsche, and Freud, we could wonder whether they are masters of suspicion or philosophers of trust. If they do not expect to find anything except for their own wish to know, to act, and to desire; do not propose any philosophical task other than interpreting the forces that guide and confront these wishes; and that, in the end, are committed to the possibility of transforming them, does not this make them great reservoirs of trust in humanity and its capacity to create itself, transform itself, and heal itself? When his lecture was opened to the floor, Foucault says (in the transcribed Spanish version) that, with them, 'la salud sustituye a la salvación', citing the original words – 'la santé remplace le

---

* Ibid., p. 274 (in English).

salut' (health replaces salvation) – of the physician and historian of science José Miguel Guardia in 1860, although Foucault gives no further reference. In French, there is a wordplay with *salut* (salvation) and *santé* (health). What it points to is the shift from metaphysics and theology to therapeutics as a practice in the hands of real men and women who, by their action, can change their ways of thinking, and vice versa. But they can do so only if they accept and understand that they cannot aspire to absolute control of themselves and the world because they are caught up in material, social, and cultural forces that go beyond them and beyond what each person is able to see.

What the masters of suspicion teach is that trust does not depend on faith or hope. There is no need to transfer belief to another field, or to the promise of something better, an expectation, or an outcome. Trust is based on our ability to relate to what we do not know and what we cannot totally control. Hence, trust is a basic social fact, but can it be regarded as a philosophical position?

Trust has been analysed as one of the founding principles of complex societies. More than an ancient virtue, it is an indispensable factor for the functioning of market societies with their money exchanges and social mobility. Locke pointed out that humans live on trust and other more recent authors have taken up this idea. From a communitarian position, Francis Fukuyama has devoted a work to drawing attention of the factors of, inter alia, family, religious, and value-based trust that continue to organise civil society based on the market and rule of law.* From the perspective of the theory of social systems, Niklas Luhmann has taken the concept further. In his book *Trust and Power* (1979), he analyses this relationship as an important factor in the reduction of complexity. Trust absorbs uncertainty and expands the possibilities for action and decision-making when we cannot analyse, monitor, and

---

* Francis Fukuyama, *Trust: The Social Virtues and the Creation of Prosperity*, New York: Free Press, 1995.

bear in mind all the variables that are interacting in a complex society. Pointing out that trust is not the only important factor in the world, he continues, 'But a highly complex but nevertheless structured representation of the world could not be established without a fairly complex society, which in turn could not be established without trust.'* From the standpoint of a functional analysis, trust enables acceptance of risk and, at the same time, learning. Luhmann argues against trusting in chaos but also against trusting in absolute order. The need for trust is the consequence of the freedom of action of other people. And the possibility for trust rests on the latent, anonymous sense that shapes the meaning of the world. It means that no relationship starts from scratch, but this is not to suggest that it is completely determined either, because there is a received basis on which to foster learning a rationality, the one that establishes the criteria for moving between trust and distrust.

But, beyond this fundamental social fact, in what sense can trust be a philosophical position? To begin with, it seems to be the very opposite of the critical, suspicious, and unbiased stand that philosophy demands as its starting point. But being situated in a critical position, being able to combat established truth, prejudices, and clichés entails, precisely, gaining a form of trust, the one that, among ourselves, only we can give each other. It is trust in our ability to construct a shared reasoning on the basis of what does not seem to make sense: our partial, fragile, and utterly singular existence in a world whose totality we will never be able to understand. This philosophical sense of trust does not depend on any higher instance, or expectation, or promise, and, still less, on any claim to the superiority of the human being as a source of sense. Like philosophy itself, trust assumes a power to act in common, which is to say in community, and starting from learning and critical reflection.

---

* Niklas Luhmann, *Trust and Power*, ed. Christian Morgner and Michael King, Cambridge: Polity, 2017, p. 103.

The New Zealand–born American philosopher Annette Baier who has devoted her entire career to studying what she calls the 'female voice' of David Hume and its moral implications, suggests that morality based on abstract principles and the ideal of justice should make way for an ethics that comes from dealing with, and from the interplay of, the reciprocities that make up the plural empirical base of any specific social life.* In this ethics, the main virtue is trust, as a concept bridging congeniality and reflection, love and duty, feeling and reason. It is an ethics that moves away from the contractual conception of political and social life to its cooperative reality as the true foundation of a community of moral apprenticeship. It is a community that does not consist of contracting parties but of vulnerable lives. Trust means accepting vulnerability to the harm that others might inflict, while also judging that they will not actually inflict harm. So, trust does not exclude exploitation and inequality but puts us in the position of having to examine the conditions for reciprocal trust in each case. Trust means exploring the conditions for trust. It is an attitude not of vigilance but of critical attention in which we agree to become dependent, giving discretional powers to those to whom we give our trust. Annette Baier asks why we need to do this and how.

Her question, formulated from the domain of moral philosophy, is at the heart of all philosophy, as a general approach. Why do we trust others to think together what each of us must think for ourselves? There is no philosophy that is valid for one person alone, but there is no philosophy that should not be thought and re-thought by each one of us. Doing philosophy is trusting that all of us have the same ability to think, although we will never think the same. It is about trusting that the reasons that underpin an idea are not just personal notions

---

* Notable among her books are *Death and Character: Further Reflections on Hume*, Cambridge, MA: Harvard University Press, 2008, and *Reflections on How We Live*, Oxford: Oxford University Press, 2009.

or fancies but collective needs that can also be revised collectively. It is about trusting that, only from this trust, would it be possible to wage a real battle of thinking against everything we are not allowed to think or, therefore, live.

This trust that does not cling to promises or expectations but takes the form of a receptive and also critical attitude of commitment to the world we share has the virtue of *unfinishing* the world, and it does so precisely because it trusts in what cannot be monitored, cannot be computed, cannot be controlled, and in that which can only be continued. Beyond a therapeutic conception of thought as – following Nietzsche – Foucault proposed, I believe that we need to develop a way of thinking that is capable of re-creating the world, by which I mean unfinished philosophy in an exhausted planet. The good life or *buen vivir* that guides all therapeutic philosophy must today tackle the possibility of humanity's self-destruction through the destruction of its conditions of life. This would entail not only trusting in thought as a community of learning about humanity's basic questions (How to live? How to think? How to act?) but also trusting in other ways of thinking that have not been part of the Western tradition, and that have not shaped this space of world dominance that we call globalisation. As I said, Europe can no longer offer answers to the problems it has posed for humanity as a whole, even when taking up the approaches of postcolonial thought. This fact points to a new philosophical situation for our times, namely the need to think together about what nobody can fix alone.